Minority Aging

and the legislative process

Minority Aging

and the legislative process

Third
Institute
Proceedings

Edited by:	E. Percil Stanford, Ph.D. Director, Center on Aging School of Social Work San Diego State University
Editorial Assistance:	Shirley A. Lockery, MSW—MPA Lecturer, Center on Aging School of Social Work San Diego State University
	David C. Pritchard, ACSW Adjunct Professor, Center on Aging School of Social Work San Diego State University
Cover Logo:	Humangraphic, Calvin Woo Graphic Design
Interior Graphics:	Pat George Graphic Arts San Diego State University
Published by:	Center on Aging School of Social Work San Diego State University
Distributed by:	The Campanile Press San Diego State University San Diego, California 92182

ISBN 0-916304-29-9

ADVISORY COMMITTEE

Mr. Peope P. Balista
Executive Director
Operation Samahan

Ms. Jessie Beresford
Director
Senior Citizens Program

Dr. Millard R. Biggs
Associate Dean, Professional Studies
San Diego State University

Ms. Grace Blaszkowski
Asian American Community Affairs
San Diego County Human Resources

Ms. Doris Block
Administrative Assistant
Councilman Leon L. Williams' Office

Mr. Mateo Camarillo
Director
Chicano Federation

Dr. Irene Cheng
Founder
Chung Hwa (Chinese) School

Mr. Jose Diaz
Administrative Assistant
Assemblyman Peter Chacon's Office

Dr. Frank Dukepoo
Assistant Professor
San Diego State University

Ms. Marilyn Halpern
Assistant Professor
San Diego State University

Dr. Wesley Ishikawa
Professor
San Diego State University

Ms. Sandra Nathan
Community Consultant
Office of Senior Citizen Affairs

Ms. Amy Okamura
Field Instructor
San Diego State University

Dr. Wilhelmina Perry
Associate Professor
San Diego State University

Ms. Shirley W. Thomas
Assistant Professor
San Diego State University

Mr. George Valle
Senior Citizen Coordinator
Chicano Federation

Ms. Beverly Yip
Director
Union of Pan Asian Communities

ACKNOWLEDGEMENTS

The preparation of this monograph was made possible by the involvement of all of those persons who participated in the Third National Institute on Minority Aging and the supportive efforts of the staff of the Center on Aging. Special acknowledgement is made to Shirley Lockery of the Center on Aging, who spent many hours in addition to her normal workload developing the program on which the proceedings are based. Kathleen Kenny, Ella Fisher, David Pritchard, and Cynthia Wright are acknowledged for the valuable assistance they provided during the period in which the Institute was being developed. Frank Dukepoo, Wesley Ishikawa, Jean Maxwell, and Wilhelmina Perry chaired major sections or served as moderators during plenary sessions. Their contributions are greatly appreciated.

The Advisory Committee that worked with the Center on Aging in planning the Institute is to be thanked for its guidance and suggestions which have made the material in this monograph possible. Most of all, the numerous individuals and organizations that encouraged us to move ahead with yet another National Institute on Minority Aging are acknowledged. It is because of their commitment and support that we were able to move ahead. In addition, the time given by several people to read through the manuscript must certainly be acknowledged. Without their help and critical advice, the content of the monograph would be less than adequate. Not enough can be said about the dedication and sincerity of those who graciously contributed their time and efforts to the production of this monograph.

PREFACE

Although great strides have been made in the development and preparation of material in the area of minority aging, the paucity of reliable and meaningful information is noteworthy. The efforts of the Center on Aging to overcome the gap that continues to exist are demonstrated by the sponsorship of the Institutes on Minority Aging. This book represents the third effort to provide administrators, planners, teachers, and students with information that may be helpful in their daily work activities.

The monograph represents a look at some of the many directions in which legislators, policy makers, and administrators have gone in developing programs and policy that may have an impact on the minority older person. The material included herein provides insights into the considerations and actions of some planners and legislators. Attention is also given to determining strategies for the future. The body of available knowledge suggests that significant changes can be made without causing major negative reactions.

Contents

vi   **Preface**

xi   **Welcome**
  James Ellis

xiii   **Overview**
  E. Percil Stanford

xv   **Keynote Address**
  Leon Williams

xix   **Introduction**
  E. Percil Stanford

Part I   **Sources of Significant Input for Legislation**

1   **Strategies for Effective Input by the Elderly**
  Jamie Jamison

5   **Historical and Current Perspectives on Legislation**
  Janet Levy

9   **Role of the Regional Office**
  Robert Schween

18   **Legislative Procedures and Your Input**
  Sherron Heimstra

Part II   **Policy Issues and the Minority Aged**

21   **Overview of Policy Issues and their Impact on the Ethnic Elderly**
  Jamie Jamison

25   **Policy and the Minority Aged at the State Level**
  Franklin R. Leslie

29   **The Minority Aging—an Action Plan for Help**
  Arturo E. Raya

34   **Social Security and Supplemental Income**
  James W. Chase

38   **Research and its Relation to Policy Formulation**
  Sharon Moriwaki

40   **The State Office on Aging and Legislative Implications**
  Stan Nielson

Part III   **Political Strategies and Considerations**

49   **Political Considerations for Change**
  Ruben Dominguez

51   **Retirement Legislation and the Minority Aged**
  Julian C. Dixon

56   **Strategies for Affecting Legislative Priorities**
  Peter Chacon

64   **Bibliography**

   Appendices

92   **Input on Legislation**
  Sherron Heimstra

95   **IMA Program**

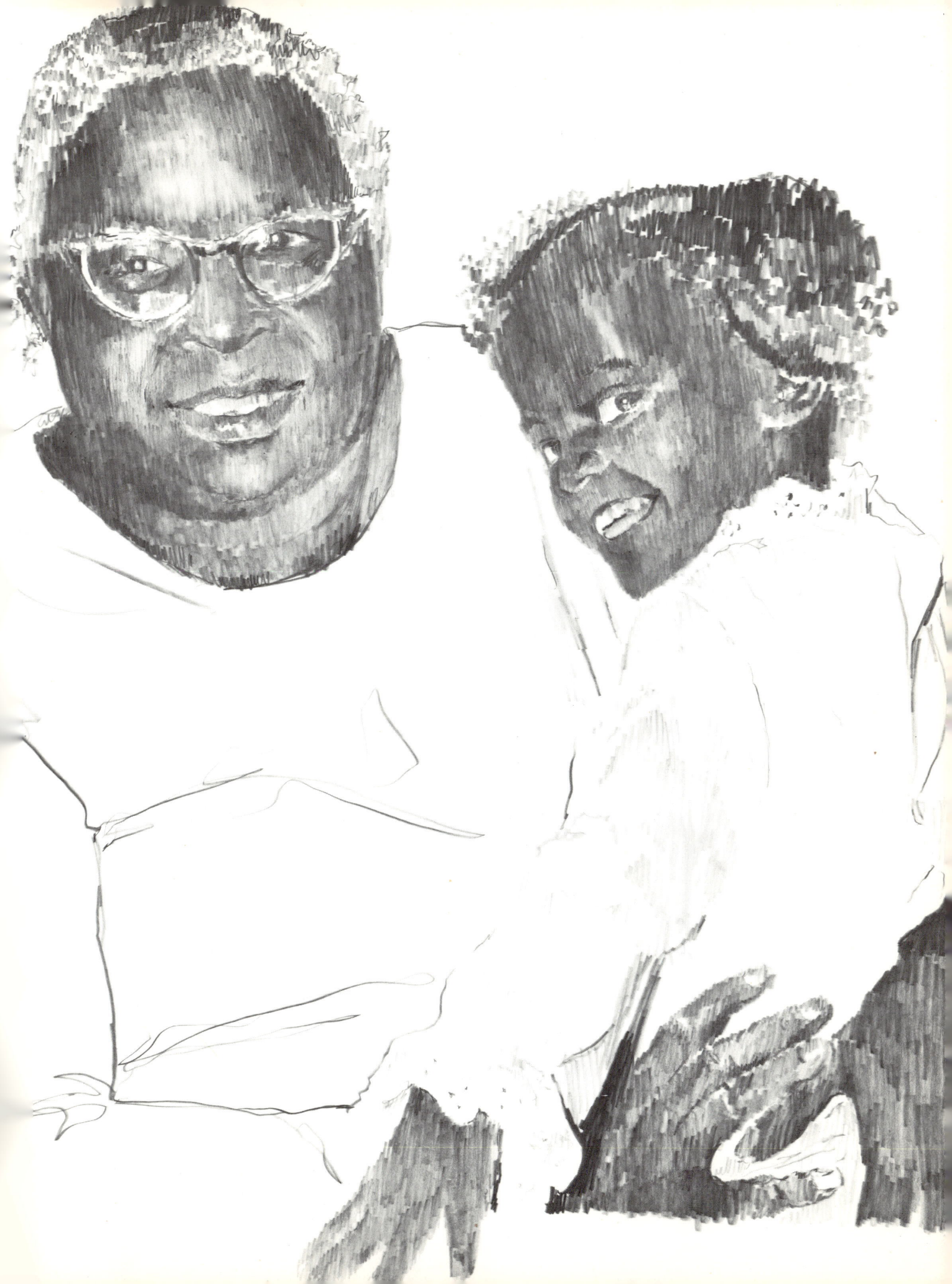

Councilman James Ellis
Seventh District
San Diego, California

It is my pleasure to represent the City Council this morning to help you open this session on such an important—and probably a continuing—occasion where all of us have a vested interest. Some of the organizations we see that have meetings and conferences and conventions and so on, are more or less single-purpose or a single idea; yours is too, but it's probably one of the few where all of us, with the grace of the good Lord, will reach that day where we could be an aged person.

The City of San Diego, of course, is one city which we feel is leading the field in public assistance in the area of aging—in minority as well as all ethnic backgrounds. You may recall recently that we approved a budget which will expand our transportation system tremendously in a Dial-a-Ride type of system. We had three pilot contracts running for one to two years; they proved so successful and so popular, and so necessary, that those three now have been combined into one and the entire system has been expanded considerably to cover about 70 percent of the people in need in San Diego. When I say those in need, I'm referring to the elderly and the handicapped. And this system will be inaugurated July lst when our new budget takes effect, and we hope it will be a great step forward and will help many, many people who lack ability to move themselves about, to get out and rejoin many of the citizens and friends that they have throughout the City.

The System is one which will have growing pains; we know we will have to work very closely with whichever agency turns out to be running it, and to monitor it very closely will be expensive. We feel it's necessary and hope that abuse will be taken out of it.

You may have read in the paper this morning where we are in some sort of a conflict with our friends, the Board of Supervisors over the Nutrition Program. We unilaterally took a step which we feel was extremely necessary in expanding our Nurtition Program to the elderly. This was met with some consternation from the Board of Supervisors and the United Way, because it was a little bit ahead of their priority list. We will continue to pursue this route that we have taken. We hope that we will not, by our action, completely destroy the Human Care Services Organization, but we felt that since the number one priority on their list was nutrition, it was certainly proper for us to take the initiative and step forward and to institute programs which we have been successful with in selected areas in the past year. So we will be working out that problem. We hope you will share our concern over the steps that we have taken. Of course, what it means is that when we allot $350,000 to that program, money will not be used in other human care areas; but we have long recognized the need for systems in the area of nutrition, particularly among the elderly folks. Many of them are incapable of helping themselves or taking care of themselves properly; they lapse into irregualr and poorly-planned meals, and we hope that this will fill that vast gap.

I have the joint privilege of greeting you not only on behalf of the City, but also on behalf of the Seventh District, which is the one I serve. You may not be familiar with our system of election, but we are nominated by our district and then elected at-large city-wide. We serve all of the citizens in the City, but, on the other hand, since we're nominated by a specific area, we generally look to our district first, and the Seventh District is that one which contains San Diego State University and United States International University. It's a tremendous privilege to be able to be the Councilperson for a district which encompasses two universities and over a hundred thousand people.

I am going to leave in a few minutes to return to the Transportation and Land Use Committee meeting at City Hall. I will be replaced here about ten o'clock by Councilman Leon Williams who is the Councilman of the Fourth District of the City of San Diego. The Committee that he is chairing at this moment is the one on transportation and land use, and is the one where the Dial-a-Ride Program expanded—had its beginning, and that Committee is very important to people in this room and to the people of the City of San Diego as a whole, because those items which we discuss, we hope, will lead to programs which we can later support and make as viable as possible. As soon as I arrive back there, I'm sure Mr. Williams will get into his car and come to you, and I think he will give a much more lengthy and detailed rundown on the problems that we face in San Diego, and some of the steps we're taking to help cure those. So once again, on behalf of the City Council, I would like to congratulate you, and welcome you here to this conference this morning.

OVERVIEW

E. Percil Stanford
Director, Center on Aging
School of Social Work
San Diego State University

It is good to see many of you here again; and for those of you who haven't been here before, we certainly welcome you to the Third National Institute on Minority Aging. I will give you just a few words about how we got started with the Institutes and then make some comments on what we are trying to accomplish now.

The Institute on Minority Aging came about as a result of the concern of many persons in the field of aging who felt there were some definite gaps that needed addressing. When we started out in the field of aging there seemed to be an implied notion that those persons who were not from middle-class, mid-American backgrounds were not highly significant in the development of the aging field in America. Therefore, historically, we find that our research, curricula, policies, etc., have been void of some of the things that would have a great impact on many of the ethnic and minority older people. We do feel, however, that in the last three or four years, some of these voids and gaps have been closing.

The first Institute in 1973 focused on five major areas. They were research, social policy, practice curriculum, environment, and health. We chose these basic areas because we felt they were the ones which people could begin to examine and take some definite steps for improvement. We found that the participants in the first conference took their task very seriously. They, in fact, came up with ideas and definite plans of action, and as a result, a monograph was developed and is being used widely by academicians and practitioners.

Our purpose during the second conference was to begin to operationalize, in more detail, some of the things that were planned or set in motion during the first conference. We focused again on research, curriculum, and social policy. The format was varied by having two other types of workshops; one dealt with consumer concerns, and another dealt with concerns of practitioners. The unique part was that we did not confine the conferees to the hotel environment; we said, if persons are interested in the practical aspects that relate to the minority older person, and if they are interested in the older person as a consumer, then we must go out and find out what those concerns are and talk with people from where they are. We had about sixty participants out in the community talking with the minority people at five different sites and we felt this was an excellent step in the right direction.

As a part of the overview, you should know about some of the things that have happened as a result of this type of Institute. When we started, there was very little, if anything, that was specific in the way of curriculum that related to the minority older person. There were some things on the horizon, but as a result of some of the deliberations and some of the thinking that has gone into the Institutes over the last two years, many people have in fact begun to develop curricula that include segments on the minority older person. The same thing to a degree can be said about research. I was very encouraged by the seriousness with which the participants approached their task in both Institutes in terms of trying to get at specific ways of approaching research that will have an impact on the minority older person. As a result of these efforts, staff from the Administration on Aging and others have begun to talk to staff at the San Diego State University, Center on Aging and to others who were involved in the Institute, to find out more about approaches to research in this area.

I can report that we are familiar with at least two or three major studies related to minority aging, and although I don't know whether there is a direct relationship, at least I'd like to think so. Another very significant activity is that some of the persons who attended the first two Institutes have begun to develop societies or professional groups that speak to their particular ethnic or cultural concerns. We feel that this is the type of meaningful activity people can pursue as a result of their involvement in these Institutes. Another benefit is that there has been more participation in and work on some of the legislative efforts at the local, state and federal levels.

The media has also become more aware of the impact and the concerns of an Institute like this. When the activities and efforts of the last two years are considered, we find that more persons are beginning to address the needs and concerns of the elderly in many communities, and are also becoming aware of the fact that there are ethnic and culturally different older pepole who must be taken into account. This is only a synopsis of some of the things that can be highlighted and reported to you today and have been important in terms of the efforts here.

What about today's conference? Many people have said, "I've come to the conference today to learn a lot, gather information, and generally increase my knowledge." We hope that is in fact true; because, if you observe the process we get involved in, there is considerable give and take from all participants and work-group leaders. The format that we've outlined for today will hopefully give you a chance to do two things; one is to listen, and the other is to ask questions and to get some of your questions answered. We're trying to involve people from the Federal, State, and local levels of government; from the private sector as well as the public sector. With this kind of mix, hopefully, you will be able to begin putting some of the process into perspective.

Too often we look at policy, legislation, and regulations, and say that there are things we have to abide by, and we do not stop to ask the question, "How did these things come to be; how could I have had input into what this is?" So, hopefully today and tomorrow we'll begin not only to address the question of "How can I have input?" but, "How is the legislative process a part of what I am?" and that is the reason for the title "The Legislative Process and You." Because it's not just the Councilperson, it's not just the Assemblyperson or the Congressperson; it's all of us. If we can go away today or at the end of the conference feeling that "Yes, I am a part of that legislative process, I can have input, and now I know how to have input," then we'll certainly be about the business of implementing some of the things initiated through this Institute two years ago.

I would like to think of the conference for the next two to three days as being one of saying "Now we've talked about the how, now let's begin to do." The other part of the conference is one which is not so academic at all. It's that part which says, we all bring something that is unique, something that is different, something that we can share with each other, and hopefully, during the next three days, we'll have an opportunity to talk with each other in very simple language, very common language about what we're doing, and about what our concerns are. Through this process, we can begin to move ahead in some very significant directions.

The foregoing comments have been intended to give you some general ideas about where we want to go as well as where we've been in the last three years. Thank you.

Councilman Leon T. Williams
San Diego City Council

I come to this conference today with many different feelings and with many different perspectives on the issues this conference seeks to explore. First, I come to you as a Black man, who has felt discrimination, from the subtle to the overt. Secondly, I come as a person who is approaching what someone else—perhaps an advertising writer for Leisure World—calls the "Golden Years" with the feeling that those golden years are likely to be tarnished. And thirdly, I come as a policy maker who finds it more difficult, especially in these days of recession rhetoric and inflation politics, to meet the pressing needs of scores of people, including the aged, because of the city's decreasing ability to pay for new programs.

My remarks today are not based on facts or figures or demographic trends among the minority aged; nor are they the result of long and scholarly research in the sociology of the senior. You are the experts in those fields. Rather, my comments this morning are the result of many years in public life. Hopefully, my observations can help humanize some of the data you've already collected and that which you may gather at this conference. Perhaps, at the end of this conference, you can help forge a means by which we can effect some positive action, particularly in legislative matters, by, and on behalf of, the aged.

To start a discussion of the legislative process, it would be appropriate to determine who it is law makers relate to as the minority aged. Any elected public official has difficulty in determining his constituency. Oh, he can say generally, he was elected by one group over another: conservationists over anticonservationists, Democrats over Republicans, and the poor over the rich. But in formulating policy in matters outside of the interest group which the elected official perceives has elected him, there is less certainty. At times, elected officials will express a vague notion of others they may represent besides their specific constituency. Countless times I've heard elected officials say, when discussing something which affects the aged, "I've got a lot of old people in my district".

Too many public officials just do not know who the aged are. And their perception of who they are is almost as faulty as the notion of how many aged may be within their districts. Two representatives may vote opposite ways on a bill, each proclaiming to represent senior citizens within their district because of the way they understand, or fail to understand, the senior citizen and his or her problems. A person representing a district containing a great number of professional or military retirees may see a greater need for property tax limitations but little, say, for food stamps. Conversely, a person representing a district with a great number of aged, who are also poor and black, will push for social legislation which will seek to have the government provide those things which make life easier.

Confusion over what constitutes the aged arises from the nature of our political system which tends to categorize people and interest groups as a means to *identify* a problem or or to camouflage it. For us that task is made easier. We are dealing with the aged minority, which is to say, for the most part, people who have generally been the recipients of public assistance, program after program, or those who have worked all their lives and can't stop now, even in old age. For them, the market place has failed. It has not met their needs. It is this failure which we must address, but which not all policy makers understand.

The aged minority of today were the poor and oppressed which the New Deal sought to placate forty years ago. For them, all the rewards of their struggle have been lost. They are still poor, still suffer from racism and worse yet, they are now old. They have even less than when they started. For many, while their children have managed to leave the ghetto, they remain. And others have come to urban centers from rural areas for services which were promised but which are rarely adequate or accessible to them.

Very rarely do policy makers relate to those on public assistance as part of their constituency. Like some statisticians, some office holders treat people like figures in a ledger book. There are more votes from the white middle class, who take the brunt of our taxing structure, than from the poor and aged. Good economics, that is cutting costs of government, has more support from the middle class than raising the level of services to the poor and the aged. Unless there is a threat of political liability in cutting back services, the public official is likely to respond more eagerly to those who are not the recipients of public assistance or social programs. For instance, the County Board of Supervisors recently cut general relief while in Washington, regulations will soon be going into effect which will give the County more money, for less work, to allegedly track down deserting fathers. The emphasis will always be, unless it can be countered by an effective lobby of the aged, on money—how much can be saved.

Meanwhile, the forgotten Americans, who have shouldered the weight, the responsibility, and the burden of where we are today have been left precious little. We are a society which puts the accent on youth and favors the new against the old. The old in our society remind us of something we do not want to see or be. Old age is at odds with our concept of ourselves as a still young, pioneering land. The plight of the aged minority is a reminder of the failure of our promise for the good life.

Occasionally the old have risen up. In the height of this country's passion for social welfare, there sprang up virtually overnight, during 1934, the Townsendite movement led by Dr. Francis Townsend. This was a significant movement because it was made up of nearly two million aged who had identified some problems of old age and had, in a spurt of self determination, sought to achieve pension reforms. Their reforms were introduced into Congress, yet when it came time to vote, 200 Congressmen were absent and those who did show up voted it down. In place of the Townsend Plan, Congress enacted the Social Security program which promised much but offered a great deal less than what the Townsendites has wanted. But Social Security looked good and a movement of the aged was co-opted by a government that was more eager to regulate the aged than to provide for them. It was the same for the movements generated at about the same time by Huey Long, Father Coughlin and Gerald L. K. Smith. Long was harrassed by the IRS. Townsend was hounded by Senate investigators and Coughlin was rebuked by his church superiors.

The legacy which we here in this room have inherited is a shameful one. The concerns of the aged today are still very much like those of Francis Townsend nearly a half century ago. And this, I believe, is due greatly to the inability of the aged to redress their grievances and to make their concerns known; not out of hope or gratitude—for 200 years has shown that does not work—but with political power things can be different!

This is easier said than done, I know. But we must begin to think in those terms. You know, there is a myth we are all imbued with from childhood, that old age brings with it grace and wisdom: the grace to accept what happens and the wisdom to know you can't change

Grace and wisdom does not put food on the table. It does not provide transportation.

It does not make life easier. Overcoming this myth on the part of the aged and the policy makers is a major hurdle to be overcome before real progress in enabling the aged to lead productive, relevant lives in our society can be achieved.

There are other hurdles which impede the aged from developing the full strength of their political muscle. There is, of course, the example of a senior citizen aide who has nothing to keep the old folks happy during the hour at the old recreation hall, but trying to get them politically involved. The first, and usually only step, is to write to a legislator. Out come the postcards and everyone writes down the sentence the worker has put on the blackboard. The result is that a lawmaker gets thirty or forty postcards, usually on the same day, with the same message: "Please vote against such and such because it will hurt senior citizens." And that's it. This approach is bad for several reasons: One, the idea is not generally their own, thus stifling creativity and discouraging original thought. Two, it instills in these people the false feeling that they are contributing to the political system and, third, the communication is of little value to the lawmaker.

I think a great deal of this occurs because of the political naivety of the aged generally who, heretofore, had really nothing to complain about, or, knew of nothing to complain about. This naivety is not limited to the aged for there needs to be a great deal more education on the political and economic system and how it works for all ages. In any case it still compounds the political inexperience of the aged.

Another reason for this political inexperience is that, in most cases, older blacks and other aged minorities are not part of the main element of the social action groups. They are on the fringe of all activist organizations which have been responsible for social change within the last twenty years.

The political power of the aged is also stifled by the emphasis of social and human care agencies toward gaining maximum economic benefits. Seldom is the power of one of these agencies focused on winning legislative battles or offering legislative solutions to the problems of the aged.

If I were to give a blueprint for how to develop political power it would be something like this:

Become educated about the political and economic process and the society. No civics textbook will enable you to do battle with the policy makers, nor with the economic forces in our society. It is not enough to know who is who on a City Council, Board of Supervisors or in the Legislature. You need to know what constituency the lawmaker perceives he is serving. Find out who contributed to his campaign and check his votes on issues which are vital to the aged. If he has voted against human care services or public assistance programs or changes in codes which aid the handicapped, he's not likely to be on your side. Find out what it takes to get him on your side.

Meanwhile, if you find a lawmaker who is sensitive to your concerns and who has, or is willing, to carry your banner in the lawmaking body, support him with accurate information and other means.

That, to my mind, is what becoming educated about the political system is.

Secondly, I would say to concentrate your strength on one issue, or a closely allied group of issues. By spreading your legislative goals too thin, you give reasons for lawmakers to shoot down the whole plan. Generally, I've found lawmakers will vote for something unless they have a reason not to. Don't give them a reason to vote against your plan On the other hand, if you're opposed to something, give them all the reasons you can to vote against it.

Unify. It's hard to fight numbers yet, if you are disorganized you may be out-maneuvered and out-voted by a smaller, less representative group.

And lastly, don't give up and don't give in. Remember others may not share your goals and the fight to achieve your goal may take a long time. If what is offered is less than you can accept, fight until you get what you want.

I am not saying these things will achieve the political strength needed to win rights for the aged minority. But I think they will put them in a better place to do so. Some things may work for one group, of course, that will not work for another.

I guess what I have said this morning is that there are a lot of myths which must be overcome before the aged are taken seriously by lawmaking bodies, and by the big economic interests. Some of these myths are within us still, but if we can see how some of these hold back the aged from exercising their right to adequate representation, we can better provide for that representation.

Until the political muscle is flexed the aged will have few victories and the legacy of our treatment of them in the past will claim yet more victims.

Thank you.

E. Percil Stanford
Director, Center on Aging
School of Social Work
San Diego State University

It is clear from the volume of legislation proposed during the last five years that legislators at all levels of government have taken the needs of aged citizens seriously. At the same time, however, they have paid minimal attention to the concerns of ethnic older people. It is also significant that older people are becoming involved in the legislative process and are much more visible today than ever before. This visibility has made it possible for their concerns to be heard in an organized and meaningful manner.

The development of a variety of organizations which work on behalf of and with older persons has also made a difference in the way in which legislators and policy-makers view them. It has been only very recently that minority older people have become more involved in the organizations and agencies working in the policy-making arena, and to take significant leadership roles in them. Heretofore, it has not been readily understood that culturally different older people have had meaningful contributions to offer. It has become eminently clear, however, that without taking into consideration the insights and experiences of the ethnic older person, legislation and new policies risk being ineffective and irrelevant to their needs.

Another very important aspect of looking at the policy/legislative process related to ethnic older people is that more specific consideration must be given to the process of how to involve those not currently involved in their own behalf. Training of older people is a necessary component in that many have not been closely involved to date in bureaucracies and formal organizations. There are many persons who have clearly indicated that if they knew how, they would be willing to participate in efforts which would lead to the development of policy which affects them. It is, therefore, the responsibility of those persons working in the various planning agencies to give the ethnic older person, and others who need to learn more about the mechanisms of involvement, the skills and techniques for becoming effective advocates on their own behalf. The skills and techniques needed are not necessarily of highly sophisticated nature. In many in instances, the information needed focuses on merely learning the appropriate source or channel to utilize. In addition, there seems to be a need for older persons to develop a higher degree of confidence in themselves because they have felt for so long that their efforts would not be appreciated or welcomed.

Policy makers and law makers in general have recently become more aware of, or, at least more accepting of, the fact that research is an important element in their work. In this respect the available material and information related to the ethnic older person has often proved to have had a negative effect. In terms of research input in minority aging, the apprehension of concerned professionals is centered around how the information is gathered and who takes responsibility for the data collection. Many researchers take the position that if they follow a scientific process there is no great need to be concerned about the cultural or individual differences in their research. In order to provide the type of legislation which will most significantly impact on the lives of ethnic older people; however, more attention must be given to the meaning of "scientific" in this context.

The scientific element is certainly important; however, where the tendency has been to dilute the significance of data because of a so-called lack of validity or reliability based on the absolute numbers or percentage of ethnic older people involved in the sample, a broader analytical perspective is in order. The important aspect of this research is that the analysis must be sensitive to the need for looking at the raw data from the standpoint of how it intimately affects the daily lives of individuals. Another very significant point is that many policy-makers have not had the inclination, and in many instances the necessary staff, to follow up on pertinent areas which may be important for consideration in their deliberations.

Ethnic older people have not had the opportunity to be heard in the same fashion or as frequently as other older people. The assumption has been that the ethnic elderly will not participate in the political process, i.e., voting. The politician has not bothered to cultivate the interest of the ethnic older people because he believes that their votes make no difference in whether he is elected. Recent trends indicate that—to the contrary—more ethnic older people are beginning to participate in the elective process and therefore are much more aware of the issues and the impact of those issues upon their daily existence. Data have shown that older people tend to continue the voting habits they have had throughout their adult lives. This may be true for many white older people, but a large number of ethnic older people have not had the opportunity to participate in the elective process. The many reasons for exclusion range from language to the complete denial of the right to vote. Therefore, it is important to look at the ways in which older ethnic people have begun to become involved, and to continue efforts to advance their involvement in meaningful ways.

Policy strategies are being discussed in the area of health and the implications for a variety of health plans for all Americans. It is vitally important to consider the health status and current plans for upgrading the quality of health service delivery to the older persons in our society. The health histories of most older people, particularly those who are seventy years of age and over, are not very well understood. In fact, in many instances, no formal record of a health history exists. In general, the health of the minority older person has been relatively poorer than that of Anglo older persons. There are several reasons for this being true. The most important of which is that most minority older persons have not had a consistent employment history to give them the economic base for providing themselves with the type of health supports associated with employment.

It is up to the minority leaders and the minority older people to continue to make policy-makers and planners aware of the health needs. There is no doubt that there is more comprehensive information needed to substantiate some of the claims made by those who are advocating better health programs for minority elders. The action must come at the planning level; if significant input is not given by the minority older people themselves, we will continue to operate in a vacuum. They can help us not only with identifying the seriousness of the health problems, but they can also provide perceptions as to the best ways of delivering health services.

Many other aspects must be considered in developing a viable policy-making process in which minority older people can participate and be effective. They must not only be welcomed to participate but must also feel comfortable working within whatever systems they choose to try to affect. Communication and language barriers continue to be a very significant part of the overall problem. Not enough attention is being paid to the gaps in communication and the misinterpretation of those things that are quite often

It is not too early to begin development of a process whereby minority older persons and those working with them might become vital links in the legislative chain. There are many real barriers to such a development; however, they cannot be cited as reasons for failure to move ahead. With the support of public officials, legislators, researchers and practitioners, matters that have an impact on the lives of older people will begin to get a fair hearing.

SOURCES OF SIGNIFICANT
INPUT FOR LEGISLATION

This section consists of presentations made by persons representing the federal, state and local levels. Discussions are focused on policy formulation and possible means for the elderly to have input into the policy development process. Panelists provide worthwhile insights as well as recommendations for moving ahead.

Dr. Wilhelmina Perry was Chairperson for this session.

Jamie Jamison
Legislative Liaison
American Association of Retired Persons
National Retired Teachers Association
Washington, D.C.

No one ever really knows when they are old—old is a nebulous thing, it's a fuzzy thing. When I go back to Cleveland, Ohio, where I was born, I talk to my father and my mother who are 75 years old and going through the same kind of pains that all elderly people are going through. My father would say," You know, Jamie, Mr. Gross down the street died the other day." I'd say," How old was he, Dad?" "Sixty-eight—a young man! " So I don't know, I just don't know when we get old, but suddenly it's upon us and we find that we have to reap the benefits of what is talked about for those who are called old.

I like working with the elderly very much; mainly because I feel that older people know all there is to know about being young, and I know so very little about being old.

We're in difficult times. Our roads are choked with cars spewing pollution. Our cost-of-living has escalated and we have had corruption at strategic levels of our government. This corruption has threatened to stifle our hearts and our spirits, and all people are suffering from the kinds of things that have developed in the past few years. But, we are in good times; odd that good times can be bad times and vice versa, isn't it?

Well, today we are gathered at the Institute on Minority Aging to discuss strategies. We are going to tie right into advocacy on how the aged can effect policy input at different levels of both the public and the private sector. When we speak of advocacy, I would like to add to that—timing. I think that advocacy plus timing can equal effectiveness. And I think the time is right. This is why I think we are in good times for advocacy. I think that the 94th Congress is prepared to right some of the ills that have beset us. I think that many of our congressmen at this point would like to prove to their constituencies, the states, and the local governments, that all of our congressmen do not cavort in the tidal basin and that when we think in terms of legislation, they are willing to support that legislation. Since January 1 in the 94th Congress, there have been approximately a hundred bills introduced that are directly associated with and have some impact on the SSI program and other programs as they affect the aged, and they are coming daily.

I came to give you some insight on how we can give input to that kind of process. I don't intend to deal with statistics on how critical housing is all over the nation, whether local, rural, urban or on the national level. I didn't come to tell you about employment and pending training programs nor that health and nutrition should be stepped up; nor do I come to tell you that all Blacks die young and that Spanish-speaking and Indian people take care of themselves through extended family tradition or that poor whites are equally as much in the minority. I feel that these general terms reflect narrow thinking on the part of many public and private officials, and because of this broad terminology, the minority constituency is discriminated against when planning programs and benefits.

On second thought, I will give you a statistic: we are in trouble. We are going to look at current legislation and try to determine at what point we as minority aged can affect that legislation so as to gain the maximum benefit. We have had the largest turnover in Congress ever. Almost all of them have gotten there by riding on the rumble seats of promises to aid the poor, the handicapped, and the elderly minority. So there they are, and here we are. Let's set about the business of the day.

The private sector about which I am to address a few of my remarks, even though I do represent federal agencies, can have stronger clout. But in touching base with federal agencies, I have an opportunity to touch base with private agencies and try to see what their attitudes, and dispositions are relative to problems of the elderly and how they can generate action.

Private agencies to this point have done some very interesting, very dynamic type programs; but I think we have accepted the small amount instead of the large amount. We have taken what was handed to us. The philosophy was that 10 percent of something is better than 100 percent of nothing. But when we take that road—10 percent of something is better than 100 percent of nothing—we do what is commonly called answering the question, but we do not solve the problem. So we should set about thinking in terms of organization to the point that we will solve long-term problems from the private sector rather than focus on questions which come today and are gone tomorrow.

As a result, I set up a chart to use as a guideline. If we follow up through our organizational structure as private agencies, we will be better able to give input at strategic levels of legislation so that elderly people can benefit greatly from it.

I'll start with research. I'm not interested in knowing how many bowls of Wheaties the elderly eat every morning, nor am I interested in knowing how many showers they take a day, but when I say research, I am talking in terms now of funding sources. I am very much in favor of getting the money first. When we speak of funding sources, let us look at the corporations. The Edna McConnell-Clark Foundation granted ten million dollars in 1974; two and one-fourth million of that money was for programs for the elderly. There are many other foundations like this who are willing to give input to the needs of the elderly and who are sensitive to the needs of the elderly. I think we should know basically who our fraternal organizations are. We should understand what role the churches can play. And we should also know which corporations have devoted their efforts to minority affairs for both the young and the elderly and which funds they have available to be tapped.

Another research strategy is for us to go to the public information sector where information lies around in the halls of Washington, D.C.; information that you can get. Perhaps many don't read the *Federal Register*; it comes out daily except Saturday, Sunday, and holidays. It tells you things such as where all the meetings are held, and gives you all addresses. Certainly I don't expect all of you to come to Washington to attend various task force meetings, etc., but you have contacts there. You may write for this information which can include minutes and the rationale. All of these things are available.

Private organizations may become a part of what is known as a bidder's list. This is the list that you can get on for every Federal organization, and they in turn will send you the kinds of proposals they are seeking. You should subscribe to the Commerce Daily Bulletin. Again, requests for proposals are there within every avenue. They may give you a broad area, but within that area you can gear to the elderly for some type of research, employment, or whatever special attack you would like to make at that particular time. The reason for this research division is to identify problems, to use it as a remedial measure, and to upgrade our own constituency. As a result, not only can we get into the initiation of legislation, but can affect it by writing and being a part of it.

The next strategy is organization. Organization—yes, it is going to be very difficult to organize, but the potential is there. At this moment, there are approximately 22 million elderly people over 65. In twenty five years at the turn of the century, the Year 2000, there will be approximately 39 million of us over 65. Don't you understand the potential of 22 million people? I say—volunteer! Yes, we are in volunteer positions now, and we are doing some great things with our volunteer programs—helping handicapped, the sick, etc. We are satisfying many, many needs. There are some other places we could be as volunteers. We can volunteer at strategic avenues of legislation. We can volunteer where legislation at the outset is being dreamed of and thought of, and we can be there while it's being done; in fact, if you volunteer as a typist, you may even type some of your ideas in.

Interpreters representing various organizations can be helpful. You know, retired people are in need of meaningful activity. Believe me, the skills we have are unbounded. We have no boundary as far as skills are concerned. We have all kinds of expertise. So when I say interpreters, I mean someone not just to read the federal regulations or to write the federal regulations, I mean to nit-pick the federal regulations. Why should something in Title XX read "and/or"? Why can't it just be a direct statement? "And/or's" give leeway, give flexibility—flexibility to back out of agreements.

Be observers—observers at hearings. Go as a body, give testimony, and if at all possible, attend some of the roll calls of the State Legislators or if you're in Washington, attend a roll call in Congress. One day, when they start to call for the votes, let your Congressman look up and look at a group of you sitting there. You'll be surprised at how quickly his position might change. It's very easy to say "no" on the telephone; it's a lot more difficult to look someone in the face and say "no".

Utilize—utilize resources. We run the gamut from laborers, to educators, to lawyers; you name it—we've got it. Utilize everything that we have so that we are getting the most for our elderly people.

Communicate! And I want to make no bones about this—write letters. I only have one thing to say about writing letters and that is we have found that the one-page letter is most effective. If the problem is written in three or four pages and gives everybody the history of it, the background—you lose them. One page—but say something. A loaded letter and support or reject whatever it is you like, or whatever it is you have decided to support or reject; but write and say it—bombard them!

Develop liaisons within your groups. Let them be around and shake hands. Let them meet certain people and talk. I'm not saying that you have to develop liaisons at the councilmen level or the congressmen level. If you can, that's great; but in so many, many cases the information is at the secretary's desk. Or information is at the administrative assistant's desk, and if you can develop the kinds of liaisons that you need, then you will get the information you are seeking.

Participate—you are doing that right now. You are participating. Participate in the legislative conferences, participate in advisory committee meetings. They are open to the public: go, listen. I attended an advisory committee meeting two weeks ago; the first advisory committee meeting of the Federal Council on Aging's Task Force on the Frail Elderly. Brand new—just getting off the ground. Couldn't even define their goals. I'm not knocking them, I'm just saying be there at the beginning to listen or have input if you can.

4   Those are the items that I have as far as my chart is concerned. We've got a lot of work to do. This afternoon in my workshop, the new Title XX will be the focus, with attention to the private sector. I intend to nit-pick it because there are some things that I do not understand, and I think there are some things that may be floating around over our heads that we really need to look at. Yes, Title XX can serve a purpose, but I think there are some things we ought to know and get out of Title XX.

In closing, I would like to say in the words of my mother, that "growing old is a bad habit . if you keep yourself busy, you won't have time for it."

Janet Levy, Director[*]
Department of Aging
State of California

Madam Chairman, Fellow Panelists and other friends of aging. For the purposes of background I'd like to give an historical sketch of what the State Legislature has done in the field of aging.

In 1951, the first California Governor's Conference on Aging was held, and from that conference the first Citizens' Advisory Committee was established. From the Citizens' Advisory Committee I drafted the legislation that created the First Commission on Aging in California. At that time we had high hopes because we already had what we called the Mini-Older American's Act and we had quite a lot to do with the early stages of the Older American's Act, especially in the area of Title III.

I think that it's also important to know that the statutes that created the First Committee on Aging in California required that the Advisory Committee be advisory not only to the governor and to members of the legislature, but to the communities. We are therefore, serving in an important advocacy role. At the time of the former commission's eight year period during one former administration, little was being done about carrying out the responsibility to the legislature and to the governor on advising what should be done in the area of legislation. At this time, 1971, two former legislative members, now Speaker Leo McCarthy and Senator Joseph Kennick, took it upon themselves to create a joint legislative committee to carry out those responsibilities. I'm giving you this bit of historical background because it gives you better insight in respect to where we are today and where we hope to go.

We have seen over 1,500 bills over the last decade, all dealing directly or indirectly with aging. Today we are covering 500 bills, forty of which are relating to minority aging. I would like to mention a few, their subject areas, and what they are all about a bit later. I want to make a very important point of the fact that we are where we are today mainly because of a few very dedicated former legislators who got in and said we have a job to do: it isn't always easy, nor is it pleasant. To get any kind of social action achieved, however, certain steps must be taken. We form alliances and we've worked very closely with the Senate Committee on Aging over the years. Through hearings, conferences and through the constant correspondence that we're getting from older people all over the state, both individually and collectively, we provide the consultant services that we hope give them more visibility and more effectiveness in their role. I think that one of the most forceful and fruitful kinds of action is to hold a hearing on a definite subject where witnesses who are brought in are able to securely and safely demonstrate the experiences, the frustrations, and the deprivations that many older people are experiencing.

I think that I should also mention that one of the first things the Joint Committee on Aging took upon itself to do was to make a priority in the area of nursing home and alternative care. One of the five statewide hearings was held right here in San Diego. This was followed by eighteen months and nine drafts of regulations to levy fines of anywhere from $50 to $5,000 for homes which are in violation of the law. To be effective, this legislation needs citizen input, concern and action. We are putting it with the law enforcement bodies of the local communities where we feel that the most effect will be felt.

I didn't mean to get off into that area, but it's a very crucial one. We are all concerned about what happens to people when they must go into a nursing home. We know that most people would prefer to stay in their own homes as long as possible. For that purpose, Speaker McCarthey has introduced legislation in Assembly Bill No. 1816 to establish a system of Senior Day Centers. These will be centers which will be multiple in their effectiveness at the community level to provide both day help, supervision, treatment, and diagnostic services; and on the other side, multipurpose activity centers for the more active older person. We're going through some amendment procedures and hearings with people who are in the senior center care business, and we hope that before very long the bill will be ready to go to the other house and come up with some substantial support.

I would now like to brief you on the important pieces of legislation dealing with minority aging.

Senate Bill 7—to provide bilingual education.

Senate Bill 52—provides for an expansion of the Indian Health Services. The original bill, which was passed last year, did not allow for private, nonprofit, corporations, foundations, as we've heard Mr. Jamison discuss. I'm so glad we are finally hearing people start to talk about some of the foundations that are there and ready and willing but just don't know enough about the needs of this field. We have to keep them well informed. This bill will open the doors for foundations and for any other kind of contributing body that wishes to get into this important program.

Senate Bill 56—provides for foreign medical doctors to take retraining and be qualified to practice in California. We have had a lot of older but very fine doctors who were not qualified come to this country from other nations. There were no retraining programs available to them and this bill will establish the program. The present law, as I said, doesn't provide for a state financed program which this will be. There's also another one, an assembly bill that I'll mention later for community colleges to do the same thing.

Senate Bill 411—provides for a bilingual phone directory and bilingual operators. There is another bill to provide for bilingual emergency operators as well.

Senate Bill 443—to write a special concern for salaries for bilingual staff. I think this is an important bill because so many times a person has this special skill and they are not being rewarded for it.

Senate Bill 493—provides for bilingual school office employees. So many times people will go into a school to get information, to get the kind of reference that they need and there won't be anyone in that office who speaks the Spanish language or whatever language it might be. This is to provide for that service.

Senate Bills 820 and 821—provide for two special commissions. The first—820, the commission on the Spanish-speaking affairs and 821, commission on Asian and Pacific Island affairs.

Senate Bill 888—provides for special Spanish-speaking interpreters in the Small Claims Courts. This is where they find they have a great many problems.

Senate Bill 963—provides for a bilingual elections act, where there will be the language spoken in that area whether it be Spanish, Chinese, Japanese or whatever. It has to be over a certain population percentage using the language in that area, but this is a very important act—the Bilingual Election Act.

Senate Bill 964—provides for court interpreters, and **Senate Concurrent Resolution 23** provides for all state materials, such as references to certain kinds of information that people need to get through the state system for a non-English listing. Right now they are all in English.

Those, I believe are all of the Senate Bills. There are a few important Assembly Bills that I would like to mention.

Assembly Bill 110—to provide bilingual sample ballots for people during election.

Assembly Bill 214—to provide for a consent form in the area under Medi-Cal where sterilization is necessary. This bill requires that the Department of Health print those regulations in the language spoken in the areas where this is being carried out. The consent form is what the bill requires to be written not only in English, but in Spanish and in the other languages as required.

Assembly Bill 860—I mentioned that the community colleges will be providing refresher courses for foreign medical graduates. The one I previously metnioned is in the Senate, and this is the Assembly Companion Bill.

Assembly Bill 1717—provides bilingual services for all state agencies, which is long overdue. This should have been done a long time ago. There have been bills to do it, but they've never been passed.

Assembly Joint Resolution 9—which is a very special kind of resolution to assure the continuance of a bilingual television program for California. For those of you who are familiar with the television show "Villa Allegra", this is done through a California nonprofit corporation, and it is supposed to be a very fine educational program for youngsters.

Assembly Bill 2204—requires affirmative action in the hiring of minorities in State Civil Service. This takes into effect the University of California, the State University and College System, and the community colleges.

I have given you all the bills first, and now I'm going to just briefly break down in numbers the older minority aging in California. The total number that are over sixty years of age is 2,600,595 Californians of all colors and all races. Of those, 15 percent or 395,544 are older minority persons. These figures are taken from population statistics compiled by the Office on Aging from the 1970 census.

I'm pretty close to coming to a close, but the thing I wanted to say mainly is that the Joint Committee on Aging can only be as effective as the older people either let it be or make it be because we're dependent upon their input, and we are as dependent as they are on our feedback to them. We do give out a current summary of all the legislation affecting older people and anyone who wishes can be on that mailing list so that they are kept informed and advised.

Discussion: Question About Senate Bill 173: This bill requires that an audiologist be called in right at the beginning of a person's hearing problems. We are desperately trying to get it passed because the hearing aid industry in California publicly is spending a half million dollars to kill the bill. Now you know who that bill is going to be good for—not for the industry certainly, but it is going to be good for the older person. This is the kind of bill we're concerned about, a bill that affects ethnic groups and people of minority origin. Incidentally, we are starting something to do away with mandatory retirement. This is not going to be easy. But the way we are starting it in California is that we have a bill to say that the retirement age of sixty-seven for state employees working in the field of aging must be eliminated. We can't work in the field of aging and say at sixty-seven, you're through. This is where we are going to start, and we hope it's going to lead to much, much better kinds of laws. Thank you very much, and I'll look forward to meeting with some of you later.

*At the time of this Institute Ms. Levy was Consultant, Joint Committee on Aging, California State Legislature

Robert Schween
Program Specialist
Administration on Aging
Office of Housing Development
Department of Health, Education and Welfare
Denver, Colorado

I'll quickly go over the role of the HEW Regional Office, and if you're more interested in any one of these things, we can discuss it in the workshop later today. Of course, one of our main functions is monitoring and accessing state plans; helping the state work with the state plan, administering and so forth and complying with the federal laws and regulations. We're heavily involved in agreements right now. Dr. Fleming has developed some very significant agreements with CETA, the Department of Labor, with the Department of Transportation, Office of Education, Action, HUD, the works—we can go into all those in the workshop. Primarily, our chief function is providing technical assistance. We hope we have some expertise; we hope we can provide quality technical assistance to the state agencies and Area Agencies on Nutrition projects, Title III, Title VII, Title IV-A, and anything that they would get funding for or any of their endeavors such as model projects, or ombudsman projects.

As far as going into management concepts, our region does a lot of management by objectives, operational planning sytems, training with staff people in states, and of course advocacy is involved. We spend considerable time analyzing public policy for whatever implications it has for our particular region, which of course is small. We do not have unlimited power in Region VIII. In New York, the State Agency has 100 employees; Wyoming has two!

As far as a minority push in our region is concerned, I think we are in a very commanding position. We have very strong affirmative action plans in all of our states, and we monitor these regularly. Montana has set up an Indian Area Agency whereby seven different reservations have combined. They have one area agency that accommodates all seven reservations. We have some really unique SSI pushers on reservations throughout our region, and we have also supported state plans being published in Spanish in Colorado, Wyoming and Utah. Other than that, I could go on for quite a while about our roles and functions in different things.

I know state people think that we expect a lot of them and we do. Regional offices expect a lot from state agency people and sometimes too much. But we think you can do it, and what's more, you've got to do it.

Sherron Heimstra
Legislative Analyst
Administration on Aging
Department of Health, Education and Welfare
Office of Human Development

You've heard a lot about involvement and commitment in your role of assisting the older person. I'm going to outline some of the federal legislative procedures and steps taken in the legislative process so you can have input. I think I'd like to go over for just a few minutes the reasons why you need to have input into these processes. Administration on Aging legislative responsibilities are in two distinct areas. First, as the administrator of programs under the Older Americans Act, we must assume responsibility for our program. And second, as an advocate and a focal point for aging concerns, we must have as much knowledge about the provisions of other programs of legislation, and as much impact on the content of that legislation, as is possible. In many ways our role in this area duplicates the one you have to assume both for federal programs and for your own state legislation.

Our policy of advocacy takes two forms. First, in areas of policy, it's very clear that there are certain areas of extreme discrimination against older persons in such programs as Supplemental Security Income, Home Health Care, health care in general, high rental requirements, loan requirements, loan policy, the agricultural extension service, social services funding and the allocation of resources under those programs. In determining what the policy areas are and where you want to impact, it is very critical that you undesrtand the intent of different pieces of legislation and, even if it doesn't explicitly say that the aging are eligible and are being involved in a program, how you can get some impact into it. This is one of the things we try to do at the federal level and one of the things that we would hope to get your assistance on, because the more voices that we have in support of the recommended policy changes, the more chance that those changes will come about.

The second area of department policy relates to funding in these basic programs. Where does the money go? You know that there is funding for education, for health, for rehabilitation, for housing, for legal services; the list could go on and on. But is the funding that's available actually used to serve the people that you want to be served? The statistics that we have today say "no", that isn't the case. For example, in adult basic education programs, 76 percent of all persons who are considered illiterate are older persons aged forty-five and above; 31 percent are forty-five to sixty, 45 percent are sixty and over, —but only 19 percent of all money in adult basic education programs goes to serve these age groups. And the split-out of those funds is 17 percent for persons forty-five to sixty and 2 percent for persons sixty and over—adult basic education. In rehabilitation, only 17 percent of funds over rehabilitation programs goes to persons forty-five and over, and you can imagine what the split there is also. The reason for this and for discrimination in many programs where you find such blatant funding discrimination is because of the emphasis of these programs on employment and the ability of the individual who is being rehabilitated or re-educated or retrained to get into employment cycles. This is one of the things that we have to break, at the federal and at the state and local levels, in terms of attitudes towards the establishment of funding programs. This is a purely qualitative philosophical question that the society has to address, and it can only be addressed if pressure is exerted from aging groups who say "look, we're citizens; you, yourself have placed the burden of mandatory retirement on us. You can't double the burden that we face there by also depriving us of services." Going on, in legal services programs, legal service for the poor is a major consideration in any program for elderly persons. One of the reasons for this is the location of the services themselves—their outreach kind of effort, the willingness of older people to go into centers where young kids are walking around with long hair and jeans. Those are the kinds of problems you're most familiar with and that you can deal with on a community level; but again, this is the kind of thing that we want to try to end. In health care older people have three times the per-capita health care expenditures in the country of persons between nineteen and sixty, but only 6 percent of the health care costs for ambulatory care (outpatient care) is provided in clinics that are subsidized by the public health maintenance organization systems trying to emphasize preventive care, maintenance care and enroll everybody. Only 30 percent of health maintenance organizations even have Medicare reimbursement scheduled. What this means, and this again has to be dealt with at the community level, is that if the Department of Health, Education and Welfare doesn't have a Medicare reimbursement arrangement, the older person can't use his Medicare cost and then get HEW to cover the other portion of care. Health maintenance organizations have been reluctant to enroll older people because they have higher health care costs which increase the cost of health maintenance organizations in terms of preventive and dental care, the immediate kinds of service they need. This is the same thing that has been experienced, by the way, by the poor in general in terms of their Medicaid reimbursement under health maintenance organizations. Very few health maintenance organizations have been willing to sign an agreement with the state to allow Medicaid reimbursement for the health care of the poor.

Clearly, these are areas where we both have to cooperate—the federal government needs your help and you need the help of the federal government. Our help from you has to come come through the identification of difficulties you find at the local level. And that includes identification of problems for the administrative executive side of government and through the congressional side. This federal legislation can be a big help to you.

At this point, I would like to give an overview of the process of federal legislation development and talk about some of the ways you can impact at various points in that development. Then I will summarize a few of the points that Mr. Jamison made in terms of stressing the specific ways that you should organize yourselves to achieve this kind of impact. The first thing in the development of legislation is of course the identification of issues. These issues can range from anything from the one-third reduction in an SSI beneficiary payment if the person is living at home and the detrimental impact that would have, to kinds of changes that you would want in such legislation as the Older Americans Act which is currently up for consideration. Because of the advantage that this legislation has in terms of whether it impacts only an existing program or whether you're asking for change in a program that's going to phase out anyway, there are several points which could differ in terms of the way that these issues would be raised and timing would also be different. In the first instance, where you would have extension of legislation, this kind of a situation would arise where a program is about to be phased out or considered for reauthorization funds; and again, one example of this would be the Older Americans Act. Our legislation will expire at the end of this fiscal year, which is June 30. Both the administration and the legislative committees that have jurisdiction over this legislation began looking at the kind of changes they would like to see.

In terms of the legislative committees, they have hearings, both in the field and in Washington, to identify problems and to get people's feelings on "OK, we're going to suggest this, what do you think about it?" Now this was last June. In January, these hearings were pretty much over, with the exception of hearings that were held in Washington, and again, these were by the legislative committees that had jurisdiction. After those hearings, then, the legislative committees would be ready to develop a bill because they would have gotten a view of how various individuals felt. If you want to get input into that process, this is where you go to Mr. Jamison's points about contacting individuals who were responsible for these various committees and subcommittees. In each case, depending on the subject areas you wish to approach, each individual is going to be different; and that is one way that Congress keeps people from getting quite as much input as they might by leaving things a little bit confusing for all of us. I still haven't figured out what the various committee jurisdictions are in all the areas in which I'm involved.

The second group of hearings would be held by investigative committees. Now the investigative committee for aging covers a whole gamut of areas. Rather than having, for example, just the housing area, which would be the case in the legislative committee area or transportation as handled by another committee; instead of being broken out that way, aging would handle housing, transportation, pension rights, SSI, a whole range of things. And they have continuing hearings. The Senate Special Committee on Aging is the group in the Senate that handles these areas throughout the year and that group has recently been joined by a House Committee on Aging chaired by Mr. Randall. And you're very fortunate here because the minority leader for that committee is Mr. Wilson from San Diego. So I would suggest that if you want to get any input into that particular group you contact Mr. Wilson.

Another method of impact is by a written testimony. You can do this as a member of an organization or you can do it as an individual and that written testimony has to be included in whatever record is kept of the proceedings we hear, and those hearing proceedings will all be published. So you've got two investigative hearings that are being held throughout the year. In terms of special concerns, there are always issues that once legislation is passed, somebody comes up a few minutes later and says, "why in the world did you do this? It's having a terrible effect on my constituents, I'm getting mail," etc.; "I'm being dropped from the welfare roles"; that they're losing their Medicaid; that they're doing various things because you've passed faulty legislation. So if legislation is passed and it doesn't meet your needs, you can go back to the legislative committee that passed the legislation. Once hearings are held, and this is usually in the House first and then in the Senate, the bill is prepared by the legislative committee responsible for the particular area that it deals with. Now usually the committee counsel for the Senate or House Committee is the individual who is going to prepare the specific word in the legislation and is going to draft out the various issues that should be considered in the development of the bill. Again I urge that you find out in each of the areas where you're interested who those counsels are, contact them, send carbon copies of letters you write to appropriate people. You don't have to write the letter to every individual, but copies certainly should go to the counsel or to the staff. Once the bill is prepared, there is what is called a markup session. There is always a period before it's considered formally where you can make comments by again getting in touch with the jurisdictional committee. The administration at this point is often requested to give comment or technical assistance, and we strongly support this because it gives us an opportunity to comment about legislation that we're going to end up administering. And, if there are difficult problems in it at that point, we would raise questions. So another avenue would be to contact the agency that would be responsible for administering that particular bill.

Again, I'm stressing the responsible agency, organization or committee, because that's the way you're going to get the most effect from your letter writing or calling or your contacting. After the markup session, in a bill that everyone agrees upon, everyone, that is, who is working on a bill in terms of the staff or the administrative people, that bill is considered by a subcommittee executive session. And at the point where the subcommittee considers the legislation, it is debated, amended, and a vote is taken. Again, each committee would change according to the bill. At the point where the full committee has passed a bill, what's known as a committee report is published. This is a little document that accompanies the bill. If there's something you think you would be particularly interested in, and if you ask a senator or congressman for that report or for a bill, always ask for the committee report if it's being asked for consideration by the full committee. What this does is to get background of the legislation of programs that have been operating in the past; it explains what's really meant by that legislation. If you look at the legislation or I look at the legislation and I don't understand it after it's passed, what I have to do is go to the committee report so if there are problems with the language in that, that's another area where you need to follow through on your contact. After the committee report and consideration by the full committee, the bill goes to the full House, where it goes on the floor.

Now, pause for a second and think about all the things and the steps that have taken place. You'll think," That takes thirty years "—and sometimes it does! In the case of our recent legislation, it took about three weeks and so depending on how fast Congress is moving, that's the time frame that you have to adapt yourself to and work within. So again, the access that you have becomes particularly important.

Now we go to the Senate where what's called the ' clean bill ', the House bill, is sent to the Senate, and they follow this whole process of going through the subcommittee, the committee and the Senate. If the Senate wants to, it can take the House bill and say" fine and dandy, we like what you've done and we're going to pass it. " If the Senate doesn't like it, it develops its own bill and goes through the same procedure, and then you have what's called a conference on the two bills. At this point, there can be no more amendments, you have to take what the House has and what the Senate has and the House and Senate Committee work out their disagreements, but they can't make any changes after that point other than for knocking out things. If after the conference there's agreement, then you go to the President for signature.

In talking about legislation, a lot of people have the tendency to drop it there and say" OK, now it's an act that's in the law, the President has signed it "... we're assuming, of course, that the President is going to sign the legislation and not say that he doesn't agree for budgetary reasons or something else that this legislation shouldn't be passed. But that is not the end, and it shouldn't be the end of your involvement in tracking the legislation or in getting your views expressed. Once you have a law, you have to have regulations. The regulations are developed by the agency identified as responsible for administering a program, and those regulations need not be to the letter of the law. You have the responsibility of nit-picking that legislation, and for going to the agency as soon as legislation comes out and saying" alright, this is what we want in the regulations. These are the considerations that we want expressed. We want to be in on your drafting. We want to be able to commenment." If it's a big issue, you can say," we want to have a public hearing on your regulations." You can schedule your own public hearing. You don't have to ask and consider these regulations. Within the agency the process for the development of regulations is the development of issue papers on either administrative or policy questions, and at this point, outside views can be reflected. Then once your issue papers are developed they go to the administrator and he chooses on pros and cons. You raised questions in issue papers in Title XX, for example, whether raw food should be a reimbursable item under the Social Services program. I commented on that issue paper, and the first time I got it, the Social Services Administration was saying" yes". Of course, this is not mentioned in the law ever, but it was mentioned in regulations. When it came to our agency, I commented that it certainly should be, and they came back and said well, we've decided that it isn't going to be. So you lose some things, but you do have a chance to comment on what it should be.

Draft regulations are prepared as a result of the decision in issue papers and are cleared through the Department. Now in our case, that is the Department of Health, Education and Welfare, and the Office of Management and Budget (OMB). There isn't a lot of support for additional funding in any program, so there are a lot of times when the administration policy isn't what the agency policy should say but what OMB has told the agency that it has to be. Outside comments help; if the agency can show public support, there is a good opportunity for going back to OMB with enough criticism of a particular decision to win.

Once these draft regulations are cleared through the Department, they're published at what's called Notice of Proposed Rulemaking in the *Federal Register*, and when they get to that stage, there are thirty to forty-five days, usually thirty days comment period for the public. These comments are sent into the agency and the agency has to show in its publication of final regulations what comments were received, whether they were considered, and why they were or were not accepted, and then the final regulations are published.

The next step after we've gotten through regulations are guidelines—guidelines are also put out by the administering agencies and are given to the state or the local agency that's offering the program. Often these aren't made available to the public although the public has a right to them and can ask for them at any time. But these actually determine the day to day operating policies of an agency.

The last step in this process is the point where you get into the question of how resources are spent and what happens at the local level and that is the implementation of the program. The state or the local agency, depending on how federal funds are sent down, has the responsibility for establishing the programs of these funds and how quickly they establish a program with these funds. There are two facets that I urge you to consider. One of course is direct services. You know when you get transportation money that some of that transportation money should be spent on the aging, and you know you have to do something about it to ensure that transportation money for capital expenditures, for example, buys buses that can serve older persons.

But there's another underdeveloped facet of legislation that I also urge you to think about and that is planning. There's an awful lot of money now that instead of going for direct expenditures, is going to agencies; and they say,'' OK, first you're going to develop a plan and you have to show us how you're going to spend the money. OK, you're responsible for how the state decides to spend its money in this area for planning. Are the elderly needs met? Are they even considered? Do you provide the facts and the knowledge and the information about the needs of the elderly persons, their locations in a community, what kind of special concerns you have, whether they have been deprived in the past? Can you provide a funding base where an agency doesn't have to turn to previous contractors and work with them and uses that as an excuse for not funding aging programs? Can you say, OK, we can do it? ''

We can provide the administrative mechanism that you need to get programs started for the aged. We're a nonprofit organization. We can do various things with this work. This is an area that's going to grow. You've seen it in terms of the CETA program, for manpower money that's going to find the sponsors now. They have to do all the planning. Their money is only 2 percent for older persons. And in labor terms that means people forty-five and over. Two percent. Now they're about to develop technical assistance guidelines, they're finding sponsors that are going to identify the needs of older persons. But, unless people in the local communities and at the state level go to manpower commissions and manpower directors, talk to them and express the needs and employment needs of the elderly, the expenditure level is going to be the same.

The same thing for social services which is going to be discussed later this afternoon. General revenue sharing—more governments spend money for capital expenditures from general revenue sharing than for any other kind of expenditure. And only 4 percent of general revenue sharing money went for social services *period* ... to any age group. So there again, I think you have a responsibility to make sure that the program is implemented in a way that will benefit your constituency.

Now, I'd like to run through the steps again, for what you should do. First, develop your priorities. This has been stressed in the past but it's critical. You have to have so much information about the areas of concern that you have, and the aging have so many needs that if you concentrate in one area at a time and consider the legislative time table that is being developed, you'll do better. Second, identify the investigating legislative committees with jurisdiction over the areas you want to be on top of—and don't forget committees like the new Congressional Budget Committee. Don't specifically stick to areas that you're familiar with and that you know really well; branch out. Use some creativity and some initiative in identifying programs. Establish contact with senators, congressmen, staff, general counsel, anybody that you can grab on the hill. Establish contact with key people in administrating agencies. Food stamps—how many people have ever talked to anybody in the Department of Agriculture about their policy toward food stamps for older persons, about the fact that they collect only half their aid, that they don't know how many older people are actually receiving food stamps? How many people have sent in comments on Supplemental Security regulations or have called and said," look, this is a really bad policy on the fact that these older persons in rural communities have to give up their land to be eligible for supplemental security income." And again, make sure that the person you're contacting both in Congress and in the Administration is the person who has responsibility for the program. When the President made an administrative decision on both Medicare and on food stamps this past fall, I can't tell you how many letters we received opposing those decisions in the Administration on Aging. We appreciate those letters, but we aren't the people who made the decision, and we don't have any control over whether it's changed. We ended up sending those letters to the agencies with that responsibility. In the case of Medicare, the Social Security Administration, and in the case of food stamps, the Department of Agriculture. But they are most effective and most timely if they go first to the agencies with the responsibility. Comment on everything that you can possibly comment on. I think one of the most effective groups I've ever seen in commenting on any regulations has been the Ohio Department of Public Welfare. They comment on everything, their comments turn things around. They are one of maybe two or three groups who send in comments a lot of times on critical issues. So if anybody knows anyone in Ohio, find out how they do it and then let me know please.

Identify federal policy making groups. If possible, get representation of the minority aged on those groups and make those representatives accountable to you. Know what they do. Know what their positions are. This is another area where you fall down. If you get representation, then know what the people's commissions are. Two of these groups are the Federal Council on Aging and the Health Insurance Benefits Advisory Council, which makes decisions on the kind of Medicare coverage and the kinds of fees that are going to be established. A new group is going to be the National Council on Aging to the National Institute on Aging, which is going to focus on research. State and local advisory councils are of course another group that's been mentioned this morning, and I understand you have a lot of representation there already.

Use the resources of aging organizations in groups if possible, such as the National Association of Retired Teachers and American Association of Retired Persons. National Council on Aging and National Council of Senior Citizens are also groups like this. The missions of groups often differ, but they have excellent legislative staffs, and they're very capably organized. They get a lot of new material. Get on the mailing list, get every possible bit of information you can from them, and you'll have some divergent positions. You'll also have the way to make a decision.

The final thing I ask you to do is to identify other human resource program interests and aging interests and consolidate your action where at all possible. It's up to us to organize and say," we don't want another library, we don't want another highway, we want you to put more matching money into expenditures for social services so that we can get more money for people in the State." That's where we need the most important strategy that you can develop. I wish you very much luck, and I applaud those of you who are going to be working with the Gray Panthers. I'm sure that you'll have very much success there, and if I can be of any assistance, please let me know.

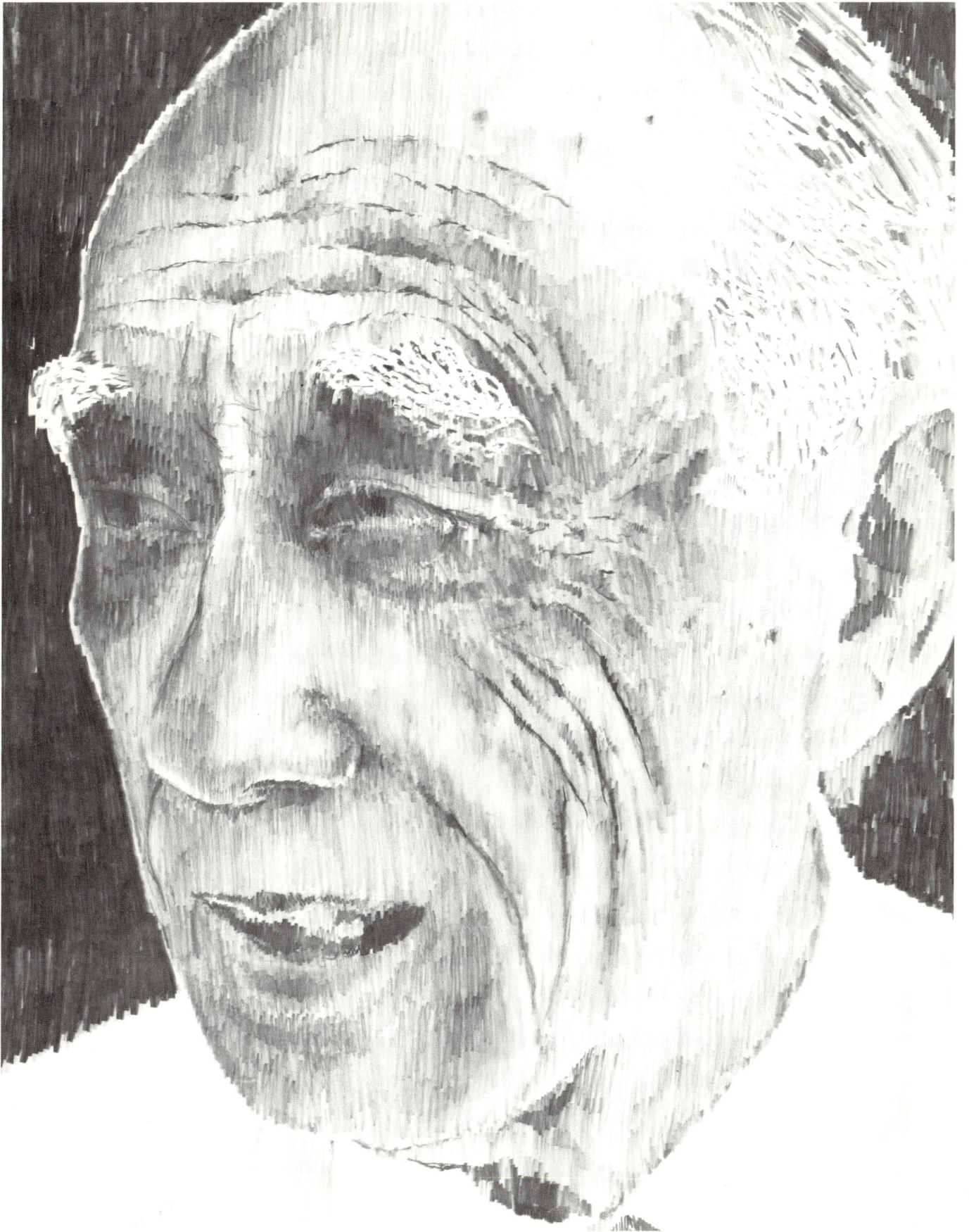

POLICY ISSUES AND
THE MINORITY AGED

Presentations in this section address some of the key policy issues which affect culturally/ethnically different older people. Attention is given to policies developing at multi-governmental levels and their potential impact on the minority older person. The range of topics is from "models for action in health" to "research in policy formation".

Professor Jean Maxwell, School of Social Work, Center on Aging, San Diego State University, was the Chairperson for this session. Dr. Frank Dukepoo, Department of Biology, Center on Aging, San Diego State University, was moderator for the panel discussion from which the material in this section was generated.

Jamie Jamison
Legislative Liaison
American Association of Retired Persons
National Retired Teachers Association
Washington, D.C.

Yesterday my last remark to you was that growing old is a bad habit and that busy people have no time for it.

I will not go into a great deal of detail on a whole lot of the legislation; the overall legislation as it exists today and where it is in Congress, but I will give you pretty much a look at what it is, what the implications are and perhaps a one-sentence breakdown of how I think it will affect us as elderly persons. Now, in our question-and-answer period, or maybe in our work-shops, we can even go into a little more detail. There are a lot of things happening. So my presentation this morning is going to be kind of like a gossip sheet and I shall touch on a lot of that, so let's start.

Recently there have been funds sought, and grants have been made in the Washington area to do a national research project on the abuse of elderly citizens by their children. It has been recorded that in our hospitals many elderly persons have come in bruised and, in many cases, have refused to reveal how they got those bruises. But there have been some who spoke, and they spoke in terms of abuse by their children. Of course, we have heard the medical terminology laid out about why kids are paying back their parents for the spankings they got a few years ago and many other things. But money has been allotted to do a study on the abuse of the elderly by their offspring.

Now, let us consider the Poison Prevention Act which originated in 1964. Out of that came safety-capped bottles to prevent children from getting into medications. Recently, the Director of Consumer Products has said that these new capped bottles must now be given to the elderly with their medication. Of course, the elderly were complaining that they were having a hard time opening some of the bottles because they could not see the arrows, match up the arrows with the slots. When they needed medication, they couldn't get it. That was also the cry of the middle-aged. Now the safty-capped or regular bottles may be gotten upon request in drug stores.

In respect to outreach, this effort is related to the United States Department of Agriculture Food Stamps Program. In Minnesota, it was brought out in the District Court that the Out-reach Program in locating food stamp recipients was not working. We had nineteen com-plaints. As a result, through the Court, the United States Department of Agirculture has ordered each state to: 1) appoint an Outreach Coordinator and, 2) re-saturate communities with Outreach efforts in order to find the many, many potential food stamp recipients who at present are not getting their food stamps. That is the Outreach Program.

In health, Gene Rubel, Health, Education and Welfare (HEW), recently gave a briefing on the new Health Planning Resources Development Act. A very, very 'cloudy' piece of material, as I see it. I have sat in on a couple of briefings on this Act. I would suggest that you write HEW, the office of Mr. Gene Rubel, to get a copy of it. It basically breaks down the nation into what is called Health Service Areas (HSA's). A Health Service Area is the division into which 500,000 persons should fall. It would be very, very important for you to know about it because governors play an important part as administrators of funds, and it is also important because HSA's can cross state lines. So it would be a matter of governors coordinating with each other. They cannot just sit back and yell and scream at each other anymore because they control their own jurisdictions. I am the first to admit that in interpreting this act, I'm still not ready to go into detail as yet. I don't feel that I am sharp enough; but I do suggest you look into it.

I also attended, not too long ago, a meeting of the full Federal Council on Aging, where they are organizing a task force to look into the frail elderly. I attended the first meeting of the Task Force on the Frail Elderly. Some of the issues discussed were populations at risk, how it would be funded, where the money would come from, would it be 100 percent free, or would it be a deductible thing. They discussed how to get housing and everything that would fall into services for the frail elderly.

I would suggest that you keep on top of the Task Force on the Frail Elderly. Just recently submitted to the full Council were tentative plans for a staff director, the kind of services they want to perform and the level of services. But as we are here and as we talk about advocacy and as we talk about being involved in programs that are getting off the ground, and as we think in terms of affecting the kinds of programs that will be very, very instrumental in the health of our aged, then these are the kinds of programs we need to look into now so that we can get the kind of input we would like.

On the other side of the ledger, there are still investigations going on within the Food Stamp Program, and the Social Security Administration is undergoing a reorganization according to the Commissioner's Bulletin. I think the most important thing is that the Cash Benefits Section will be undergoing a change, and cash benefits is basically what we are about. There is a small investigation going on in Supplemental Security Income. The Civil Service Commission is being investigated. They are looking very, very closely at the hiring practices, their inability to look at seniority and how people have gotten certain jobs in all of our governmental agencies. All of our governmental agencies are under investigation for the same kinds of programs.

I mentioned yesterday that I thought we were in difficult times. At the same time I said that I think we are in good times. We are in difficult times as we relate it with things that have happened to us in the past couple of years, but at the same time, we are in good times when we speak in terms of advocacy, and again I tie advocacy in with timing. I think the time is right.

Revenue sharing: Approximately 30 billion dollars—is winding down for Fiscal Year '75. Congress is in the process, or someone is in the process, of trying to get 40 billion dollars for this year. There are many, many gripes that affect the aged and the aged minorities, and as was brought out in one of our speeches yesterday, only 4 percent—only 4 percent of that money went for social services. I've heard all kinds of stories, and I'm sure you have too, stories about building court houses, jail houses, unplugging the sewers, street lights, capital gains. Now, of 30 billion dollars, we reaped only 4 percent of that money. We got ripped off and that same possibility still exists. Congressman Rangel of New York has come out strongly in favor of monitoring revenue sharing funds. He insists, and rightfully so, that these funds have been allocated, awarded to the states, etc., with no accountability, with a free hand operating. We must look at revenue sharing because revenue sharing can be a real asset to some of the things we are trying to do. But we must bird-dog it, we must sniff it out at the beginning and bird-dog it right down the line to find out just where the funds are going to be allotted or how they're going to be used. I suggest you make revenue sharing a priority on your list of things to do.

The Consumer Advocacy Agency: S200 has just passed the Senate and is going to the House for hearings. I don't think our President is in favor of a Consumer Advocacy Agency. He has refused to support it in many instances, but that is where it is—heading for the House.

The Older Americans Act, at present, is sitting in the Senate and is heading for mark-up.

No-fault Insurance: President Ford is opposed to this. Hearings have been held in the Senate and Congress, which are now on vacation, and the hearings will be resumed on June 5.

Credit Discrimination: It has been reported in the House and is being held up. We're getting some weird kind of opposition from one or two of our Congresswomen. The retail stores are a little upset because it appears that there have been no compromises set forth. Now, one of these is that they can conduct, or they can deny women credit based on their own evaluation without having any follow-up as such. It has been opposed by special interest groups, and I think that between the two, they're kind of at a lull here. I don't know what's going to happen to Credit Discrimination at this moment. It was designed for the elderly in order to obtain credit, but until something is resolved, that particular aspect of credit discrimination is going to be kind of waving around out there.

Title XX: Just a reminder, it has great potential with some changes. Yesterday we nit-picked Title XX in the afternoon; nit-picked sections—the language, the terminology, and some of the aims it described. We broke down the ideas as to why certain sections would be ineffective. I have left some mimeographed sheets out on the table pretty much discussing the things we talked about yesterday in our workshop on Title XX. However, I think it has a potential. We have until July 1 to make input at the state level, and I suggest that we set about the business of looking into Title XX.

Community Services Administration, formerly Office of Economic Opportunity (OEO) is operative. We should look very carefully at that to see how we can convert and expand many of our programs from the Community Services Administration. There have been hearings which were held late in November.

Housing Urban Development (HUD): Rural housing is becoming a problem because of the lack of funds that have been kicked into the possibility of rural and subsidized housing. Rural housing is becoming a very big issue as of late because of the demands of people to live in areas less prone to the high cost of taxes, etc. Rural Housing can be very, very instrumental in easing how many of our elderly live. I think that we should look into the hearings on Rural Housing. It is being sponsored by Congressman Hathaway of Maine who has taken this subject under his wing.

Also under Housing: many of you have used your GI Bill to purchase homes. Under the Veteran's Act of 1975, you may now reuse your GI Bill to purchase a second home. What you must do is not have your first home anymore; that is, you must sell it or it must be in a state of transferral where someone else has the opportunity to assume the payments, etc., but you are not liable for it anymore. You may say that this GI Bill has been reusable before; yes, almost. Before the Veteran's Act No. 94569 just passed on January 1, a veteran could reuse his GI bill to buy a home in another area, but he had to have—and it was written in the legislation—what was called a compelling reason. The compelling reason clause has been deleted in the new act. It means if you have a home and you want to sell it because taxes are too high, or you want to move away to another area and get another home—then you may look into the GI Bill. One of the drawbacks would be that the most the Veterans Administration will insure for a home is $17,500. In case you did find a home that may cost $20,000 you will have to take up that $2,500 in insurance from another source. We have found that many of our people are very, very receptive to this, those who can afford it; very, very receptive, especially in moving away from some of the areas where they lived and moving to some of the warmer areas into smaller houses. Many of our children have grown up, gone way, and the four-bedroom home is not needed anymore.

Property Tax: I think we need to look into the tax relief structure. It is absolutely depressing to read about the number of our elderly who for 35 to 40 years have paid on time mortgage payments monthly with their goal to have their house paid off, so that at retirement they could sit back and relax. It just hasn't worked out that way. In a recent story from Montgomery County, Maryland, which is a very rich county equivalent to Westchester County, New York, people had to give up their homes because they could not afford the property taxes.

It comes back again to our mandatory retirement clause. People are forced into retirement who have so many things to give—so much, not only inspiration, but so much expertise—but at a certain age they are booted out of the department. Benjamin Franklin Bailar, our new Postmaster General, is now coming up with a program where he will retire postal employees early so that he can infiltrate the Post Office with younger employees for better action plans and better services. At the same time a lot of people will be forced into mandatory retirement which again comes back to that possibility of little, no or not enough income; and we find ourselves at the short end of the stick again looking for legislation that will help us when actually we have earned it over a period of years, and it's not ours to have.

Franklin R. Leslie
Legislative Analyst
State Office on Aging
Sacramento, California

I am here to talk on legislation, but there are so many other things I feel have to be said. That Legislation should be all sorts of things can suffice with very little explanation.

People in America are organisms seeking satisfaction through adjustment, and as a person ages the need for adjustment increases and emphasis shifts to survival rather than contribution.

The reality of this fact in regard to our aging citizens is that as aging begins, vocational obsolescence may begin to develop, families may split into small groups, the mobility of those persons may become limited, and adequate housing and needed services may not be readily available. These could result in personal dependency, loss of identity, social segregation and loss of the familiar. When a person is old he is treated according to a set of culturally defined expectations of role and behavior. These may be as constraining as low income and declining health, which reduces mobility, capacity and alertness.

We are all here today because of a common interest. We are aware of the problems with which our elderly population must cope and we are all desirous of modifying those problems to assure optimum functioning of our aging citizens in their own environment. We are here because of our desire to meet the needs and provide necessary services for elderly persons, especially the minority segment of the older population. This is a meeting of persons interested in the goal of developing plans for accomplishing this mission; we hope to resolve these problems in part.

Who are we talking about? The typical 60-65 year old was a teenager during the depression, 25-30 years old during World War II, and 30-35 years old during the post-war period of economic improvement. For up to 30 or more years employment in production labor or in services, and not too infrequently long periods of unemployment, was the lot of this group. Retirement or job loss due to economic setbacks has resulted in this group being recipients of SS or SSI, neither of which is related to the economic reality of living.

The youngster who went to work at age 14 in 1900 or 1910 could not normally expect to be capable of full-time employment past age 40 or 45 at the latest. The youngster of today goes to work at 18-20 and can expect to be capable of full-time employment on most jobs to age 65.

The problems of the elderly minority today are the problems of the young minority. Every group migrating into the urban society during the last century has had to jump an educational and opportunity gap which becomes wider with each generation. When the gap was only a few weeks schooling in the 1800's, from a background of total illiteracy, it has become a matter of 12-16 years schooling in many instances. Minorities such as Mexican and Black and Asian and ironically Native American, the most recent immigrants into American society in numbers of great significance, are hit particularly hard. Social and political gains made during the thirty years between World War I and the Korean War are in grave danger as during this period gains were made as a mass production or service worker. Work has now been shifted to a knowledge foundation.

Reform regarding the elderly population is faced with disenchantment, partly due to the fact that some feel no improvement has been made, that in both cities and rural areas the elderly still live in isolation and sometimes squalor, victims of loneliness and the ills occasioned by isolation and poverty; part comes from the poor minority segment that has not benefited from programs and expenditures; and part comes from opinion leaders and others who feel there is a strong platitudinous rhetoric of vague democratic goals in contrast with reality.

Programs run by middle-class professionals have evolved so that middle class people may have benefited the most. An appropriate response might be, "Let the poor and minority frame their own proposal," but the answer is not that simple. For one reason the poor and minority have been surrounded so long by the rhetoric of reform that they may adopt hand-me-down programs which are no more applicable than proposals of the middle class. For another reason, resources are limited and goals of improved health services, housing, etc. are sought by poor and minoirty as well as those who are well off. A third reason why the minority and poor cannot be left to do the tasks is that they are a minoirty and can achieve little without support of the majority. National leadership has attempted to redirect the focus so as not to set up administrative monuments through legislation, funding and staffed programs, but to convene appropriate groups and develop suitable courses of action. However, although the amended Older Americans Act and federal policy mandate utilization of elderly and minority people, they are not not always available; at least they do r appear to be used to any extent in federal, state and local programs administration.

The local Area Agencies on Aging (AAA) were created, theoretically, to permit local control, and to an extent it has helped. I don't know how much. Resources and services have to be responsive to the users in the area, and I believe this area concept is good. The decision must be close to the people it affects and should reduce the social biases and class biases. I'm not going to say whether it actually does or not. I will say this: the minority elderly actually will never achieve a fully normalized life until they have a vested interest and authority in those parts of the bureaucracy to which they are subject.

I have a few words for the elderly in regard to legislation because they do know what the problems are and they are really citizen experts.

1)   Because you know your problems better than anyone else you are a citizen expert. Build organized support and document your problem with evidence and photographs.

2)   Learn how your community makes decisions that may affect you. Find out what is being planned.

3)   Arrive at a plan by raising issues, asking questions, posing solutions.

4)   Be a watchdog on implementation.

5)   Judge effectiveness of programs and convey your impressions to responsible parties.

6)   Early in legislative sessions, start to write or see your assemblyman and senators and give them your views and ideas and concerns.

7)   Keep abreast of bills introduced which affect you. The Joint Committee on Aging tells you what bills there are that affect elderly. CRLA is another great resource, to an

extent the Office on Aging is another resource, although it may not have as comprehensive a listing as the two other agencies.

8) Attend legislative policy committee hearings when you can or send delegates, especially on bills that may have large consequence. Convey your concerns to AAA and Administration on Aging (AOA). Contact your legislators and advise them of your support or opposition. I think that the elderly should attend some of the committee hearings on legislation relevant to the elderly. If there are bills which tend to have a big impact or would tend to have a big impact if passed, I think they should attend or at least send a delegate. I found in my hearings with the legislature that they are people like you and me. They are doing a job—they are anxious to please—with both altruistic and selfish motives. Many of them want to do good for others and others want to do good so that they can have a good record and be re-elected and this type of thing—very smart and I feel that there isn't enough activity in that direction. They are very susceptible to suggestions. Most of them are anxious to do things that would please and help their constituents. Write your governor.

9) Get copies of bills from legislators or bill room and ask AoA, AAA, etc.

Nearly all minority population growth is in ghettos rather than in rural and suburban areas. Non-white elderly continue to be concentrated in central cities and few programs are aimed at altering this tendency. Each ghetto contains a full range of poor and nonpoor, radical and conservative, economically dependent and self-sufficient. No single improvement strategy can resolve the issue as needs exist for all the elderly.

Listed here are what I see as some unresolved problems and I'd like for all of us to think about and arrive at some way of beginning to solve these problems.

1) **The record of service** in reaching the elderly is increasingly under fire and the watchword is "outreach." As the range of services is increasing, so is their complexity and outreach may be becoming more difficult. You can't get the services to the people unless they are desirous of receiving them. Outreach sounds good but many of the members of minority groups are not necessarily susceptible to the same techniques and tactics of being reached. I think that the elderly themselves, especially those of the various minority groups, are the only ones who really can effectively do anything in regard to outreach.

2) **Poverty** among the elderly is often hidden, locked up in the intercity neighborhood and isolated in rural areas. Moreover, it is interlaced with assimilation of minority groups. Effective leadership and funds are needed but that alone cannot resolve the problem. What's the answer? How can we resolve these types of problems?

3) **Labels** such as 'old' or 'elderly' point to some visible feature or incapacity and sometimes magnifies it out of proportion. When such labels accumulate others such as ethnic, racial and economic, the problem of meeting need does become complicated but the needs can be met. Attach a label to a person and a certain set of expectations follow. If this label is 'elderly' you set forth certain characteristics and certain things are expected. It's aggravating when you add to that label other labels such as 'Black', or 'Chicano', 'poor', or 'uneducated' and it has a multiplying effect, so we're really talking about a compound problem. We're really talking about dealing with this elderly minority group with the label attached. How do we cope with this?

4) **Customs for sharing** have not been entirely lacking in even the most primitive societies. In a society where few reach old age or where those who do, continue to work for income or retire on substantial and secure income, problems will not be complicated by economic factors. How can we meet more of these needs for persons not economically secure?

I'd like to say this, that the Office on Aging in action is responsive to suggestions and to questions from you the public and from the legislature. I don't feel that we really get adequate input from you. We don't know what your concerns and problems are, and I feel that it would be beneficial if the elderly were to appraise the Office on Aging of what they see as problems that need resolutions. I think the same thing would apply to the legislators as well. I have talked to many of them and have found that they are really not aware of the problems that confront the elderly or the minority elderly. Of course policies which are developed by the State Office on Aging would tend to be broad because they must be applied on a statewide basis. However, there are instances where specific solutions are necessary for a particular locality. We have to know what the problems are. Our field staff, the Area Agencies on Aging or our Director will respond and endeavor in every feasible way to cover objections, resolve problems, or suggest ways you can aid in the resolution of problems we cannot handle. Only through this kind of input can policy emerge.

The state attempts to ensure affirmative hiring policies in local programs and encourages the hiring of capable older and minority persons. Ostensibly, equity is a reality and programs and employment benefits go to those who can benefit the most. Monies are allocated and programs funded on basis of not older population only but on the basis of the incidence of low income and the percentage of minorities included in the total.

Arturo E. Raya
Associate Regional Director
Los Angeles County Department of Health Services
Central Health Services Region

We are, I am sure, all aware of the medical advances that have been made during this century. In consequence of these advances, the population group aged 65 years and over is increasing, and by the year 2000 it will number about 25 million. This achievement, while desired and welcomed, nonetheless meant something of a crisis for a society unprepared to accommodate such a burgeoning of the group of older Americans.

Today, most of America's aging, particularly the minority aging, are family members with the full complement of roles, relationships, needs and challenges that belonging in families involves. According to recent nationwide studies, four out of five older Americans are members of families. Only 20 percent of men and women over 65 are virtually kinless in America today. According to November, 1971 data from the United States Bureau of the Census, only 2.1 percent of the women 65-74 years old, and 2.3 percent of the men between 65-74 years of age were institutionalized in 1971. Even among the very old, above 75 years of age, 8.1 percent of the women and 6.0 percent of the men were in institutions of any kind.

The great majority of persons over 65 years of age live in families. Four out of five men (79.7 percent), and 57.6 percent of all women over 65 in the United States are classified as family members. Most of these older men and women are married and living with their spouses; some are making homes for their adult children; others are single women providing for their relatives, in many cases their elderly parents. In 1971, 4,500,000 men (8.33 percent) and 4,274,000 women (62.3 percent) between 65 and 74 years of age were heads of families.

Many older persons of both sexes prefer to maintain their own homes as long as they can. When they are physically and financially able to do so, older men and women enjoy the privacy, freedom and independence that living in their own homes provides them. Some 15 percent of the men and 36 percent of the women over 65 in the United States were maintaining their own homes. Two out of every three older families own their own homes, the great bulk of them free from indebtedness, with their mortgages paid up. It is not unusual for spiralling property taxes, and higher costs of living on fixed incomes to necessitate giving up the homes older persons have spent lifetimes paying for, in order to cut expenses. Unfortunately, this robs the minority elderly of their hard-earned independence, and in some instances makes them a burden upon family members, or the community at large.

In recent years considerable time and money has been spent on developing programs in various areas of aging related to the categorical view of older persons as an entity, regardless of background, experience or future outlook. There is enough general information and knowledge available to begin to look at older persons as individuals and further, as individuals with specific life styles and experiences. The efforts, though sincere, may have been less taxing and frustrating had planners allowed for diversity and differences in life styles.

Evaluation of the action taken during the last decade reveals that, in spite of great strides, progress has at best been sporadic and its momentum slowing. There is still no comprehensive set of national policies on which all levels and parts of government are working together to articulate. Older people are increasingly disadvantaged, and at least a fifth are still in the desperate, life-destroying circumstances of dire poverty.

Inflation is continuing at such a rate that, while money incomes of millions of older people were raised through increased Social Security benefits, many persons are now relatively poorer. Employment opportunities for retirees did not materialize to enable them to earn additional income. Taxes, especially property taxes, climbed to such levels that many older homeowners are being forced to sell and move into cheap rented quarters. Production of new housing for the elderly has lagged. Health services remain fragmented and uncoordinated, resulting in poor delivery of services to the elderly. Institutional care was increasingly allocated by public agencies to the proprietary nursing homes, which admittedly still need stronger regulatory measures to improve their standards.

Now, under the Older Americans Act and its implementation strategy, the Administration on Aging has adopted the following as a 1974-78 goal: to assist older persons throughout the nation to live independent, meaningful and dignified lives in their own homes or other places of residence with emphasis on the reduction of isolation and prevention of unnecessary institutionalization.

CALIFORNIA GOALS AND OBJECTIVES

State and local agencies of aging. Program efforts will proceed from an overall, uniform strategy which provides the state and localities with a planning mechanism directed toward the identification of older persons' needs or services, availability of resources, establishment of objectives and priorities, development of plans for service systems, and the development and implementation of those programs and services determined to be necessary in relation to the goals of independent living, reduction of isolation and prevention of unnecessary institutionalization.

Sub-state agencies on aging under the sponsorship of State Agencies on Aging are responsible for developing, implementing and evaluating a comprehensive plan for services and programs to serve those elderly most in need. The services to be provided under this area plan include nutrition and a wide range of other supportive services, depending on the particular needs of the sub-state area.

Service providers led by the Area Agency on Aging receive primary emphasis in the development and delivery of such services, by using existing services and organizations to the extent possible. Area Agencies on Aging will use Administration on Aging funds to fill gaps in services by funding the expansion, improvement, and/or start-up of services for the elderly by service providers.

This state and local joint effort, then, provides an element which can be included in the development and implementation of an Action Plan for Health.

VIEWS ON THE MINORITY AGING POPULATION

The health and social problems of the aging minority population are aggravated and long standing but have only recently become the focus of national attention and action. Minority leaders and their advocates have been instrumental in creating this new awareness and understanding of their peoples' needs. We stress the need for more comprehensive data on such elemental questions as the number of aged minority group members in different parts of the country, vital statistics and health data, employment status, income distribution and identification of the reasons for their low access to comprehensive health services. The spokesmen of the minority aging community are calling for direct action in these areas in order to plan for and provide adequate levels of service.

Improving the health of Americans, including the aged minority American, lies not so much in discovering new cures as it does in making available and accessible to everyone an adequate level of health services based on existing knowledge. I believe this, and I hope the participants in this meeting do too. In the past five years, a variety of social programs have been established to introduce new ways of distributing health services more equitably, effectively, and efficiently. However, these social programs, especially comprehensive health services, are still not reaching the minority aging American to the full extent of the actual need that exists for such services. The need for improved health services is reflected in higher rates of mortality and chronic health problems, in part compounded by a fear of hospitalization and removal from the family setting.

Lack of personnel capable of communicating with minority aging Americans—On every level of a patient's transaction with the public agency, patients are delayed or denied services if they do not speak English or if their social and cultural life style is different. Agency personnel often feel that they are working harder for the minority aged patient than for other patients. How else can one feel, if an interview takes twice the time it should? Moreover, there is little social work follow-up, continuity of care, health education and specifically preventive education being performed.

Comprehensive health services programs are generally less helpful to minority aging Americans than to the rest of America's poor. There are a variety of cultural, legal, and linguistic reasons for this. First, minority aging males are reluctant to seek public help because of their pride, customs, traditions, and social attitudes. Further, those coming from a folk culture—and there are substantial numbers, particularly among Spanish speaking—are accustomed to solving their own problems without seeking outside help. Many are denied benefits of various health and social programs because they are aliens.

HEALTH CARE ISSUES WITHIN SOUTHERN CALIFORNIA

Proper health care remains a very elusive goal in Southern California particularly for the area's aged. Despite the assistance of Medicare and Medi-Cal, health care and health maintenance remain the single most important problem for the aged. The effects of rising costs are often aggravated by inefficient financial and administrative systems and by the shortages of facilities. Inadequate facilities are sometimes the major barrier, yet more often it is the inefficient health care delivery system and the lack of means to pay.

Special medical problems—For all age groups, heart trouble, cancer, and strokes are the major causes of death, and nutritional problems are found at all levels. However, in comparison with those under 65, the aged are ill with greater frequency, they more often experience critical illness, such as cancer, and they require longer time for recovery according to the Bureau of the Census report, "Projections of the Population of the U.S. by Age and Sex— 1970 to 2020." For example, the diseases-of-the-heart death rate among the 65-74 is 23 times as high as that among those aged 35-44. Moreover, 86 percent of the 65+ have chronic illnesses, mainly arthritis, hearing impairment, and digestive disorders, while 72 percent of those 45 to 64 are similarly affected. Many aged are also afflicted with varied mental and neurological conditions which are often classified under senility.

Facilities: deficiencies of health facilities and personnel are mainly matters of uneven distribution within the counties of Southern California neighborhoods with low incomes, or high concentrations of minorities are shy of services as are many rural areas according to "Occupancy Rates for Acute and Nursing Care Facilities" data of the Area Comprehensive Health Planning Agencies.

The problems of access to health care include transportation where a general lack of public transport exists, but also inadequate access in central city ghettos and barrios is more a function of low income, of the unwillingness of physicians to take Medicare or Medi-Cal patients and of the fear, often associated with age, of medical care.

Lack of public transport effectively isolates medical services from the aged in rural areas or in small cities, except perhaps in emergency cases.

Multiphasic health screening services represent a type of health care with usefulness to the aged which can be greatly enhanced through better access. However, screenings without follow-up are ineffective in solving identified problems, yet follow-ups are limited by lack of access. As one health interviewer described it—you tell an old man he has cancer, and don't follow-up, he just goes home to rot.

Long-term care is a major problem for the aged for they require more long-term care than younger people. This relatively greater need arises from a combination of physical weakness and higher susceptibility to chronic and degenerative diseases. In 1971 the utilization rate of nursing care facilities in Los Angeles County among persons 65 and over was almost fifteen times as high as that among people under 65.

In all Southern California counties considered by a recent Southern California Research Council study, except San Diego County, the number of long-term care beds appears adequate to serve current and predictable future needs.

ADDITIONAL PROBLEM AREAS FOR THE AGED

1. **Stress and its effect,** often related *not to* physical deterioration, but from stresses which often accompany advancing years and result from anxieties of life.
2. The problem of **nutrition** as related to the aging process is as yet imperfectly understood. California data is very sketchy.
3. Since the aged are always on the brink of injury or illness and since they are more susceptible to catastrophic illness and chronic conditions, their **health expenditures** are, on the average, over 275 percent as large as the general public.

POSSIBLE SOLUTIONS TO CONSIDER IN AN ACTION PLAN FOR HEALTH

a. **Home Health Services:** With services directed toward achieving and maintaining a state of good health which can be provided within the physical and personal resources of the home. These can be provided by hospitals, community-based agencies, community controlled organizations or local health departments.

b. **Improved Medicare and Medi-Cal benefits.**

We agree with those who believe that adequate health care should be available and accessible to all segments of the population and that lack of income should not be a barrier to good care for particularly disadvantaged groups such as the minority aged; access requires both adequate facilities and financial support.

In the development of an action plan—national or local in scope—**alternatives to explore** are widely varied and include at least the following:

Training of Home Health Aides
Financial Support of Home Health Services
Financial and Manpower Support for Intermediate Care Facilities
Eliminate three-day prior hospitalization requirements under Medicare and Medicaid
Eliminate co-payments and deductibles under Medicaid
Eliminate reimbursement differences under Medicare and Medicaid

State and Local

Curtailment of building new acute facilities except in areas of demonstrated need
Conversion of surplus hospitals and skilled nursing facilities into ICF-HMO or some health facilities in areas of shortage
Establishment of clinics on wheels—these could be federally assisted with participation by local organizations
Establishment of scheduled patient transportation for elderly to treatment centers
Standardize Medi-Cal forms and processing
Establish gerontological units to coordinate the various service and program efforts locally
Establish and/or enlarge training efforts for home health aides at junior colleges

In my view, the development of an Action Plan for Health as it relates to the minority aging population will require an on-going effort in a changing political and economic climate. The effort will require continuing support and direction by institutions like the Center on Aging as well as participation and continued surveillance by the minority aging population itself.

James W. Chase
Social Security Administration
HEW Region IX
San Francisco, California

Social Security represents an administration or agency responsible for providing money to those people eligible for various reasons. Social Security, as you know, has been up to now more of an earned right program than anything else. You're aware of the fact that we had a very heavy program providing benefits for the aged, survivors, and disabled people in our population, as well as Medicare benefits. However, with Supplemental Security Income (SSI), we came into a brand new era that provided a different approach towards income maintenance for the general population. And as a result of this approach, we got into a situation that has become one of the most complex programs—as described by many echelons including the president—since the institution of Medicare back in 1966. I'll try to give you a little bit of background as to how SSI actually came into being.

Prior to 1972 there was a great flurry of activity nationally as we began looking into the so-called ' welfare mess ' in an attempt or an aim towards coming up with a flat floor of living, a level of living, a flat amount of benefits that could be paid to those people who were needy, who were unable to support themselves, and who did not have resources put aside for taking care of themselves. The idea was that the government would help take away some of the welfare ' stigma ' by federalizing these programs and by also providing a semblance of dignity for the people who would have to exist on these types of benefits. Then the difference in the financing was a substantial departure too, because as you know, your taxes, as far as Title II benefits are concerned, are put into special trust funds. You receive benefits when you're eligible to retire or become disabled; or if you die, your survivors may be eligible for benefits. Medicare also comes out of one of the trust funds. Anyway, all those monies come out of the special trust funds invested in the government interest-bearing securities. The departure with SSI is that the monies used for the program, for the payments made through the program, come from general revenues maintained by the federal government; in other words, out of your income tax dollars. The ideas I think germinated for quite awhile among a number of planning groups called Family Assistance Planning, that were established prior to 1972. However, there arose a debate in Congress, and there was quite a division on the issue of taking all the welfare programs and federalizing them. But suddenly at the last minute, Congress turned around and decided to take only the so-called "acceptable group of welfare recipients" from the states and to federalize that part of the program. The definition of "acceptable" was those people who could not care for themselves, and who would not be looked upon by the taxpayer as burdens in the same way as the other parts of welfare. So in effect Congress split off the aged, blind and disabled, and put them under the federal government but left the rest of welfare with the states; the rest of welfare being primarily women with children called AFDC (Aid to Families with Dependent Children).

With that approach, we in Social Security were given the job within a very, very, short time frame of trying to put together regional staffs and district office staffs, sufficient to address the new problem we were facing. The legislation was passed on October 30, 1972. By January 1, 1974, we had to be in a position to actually send out the first checks under the SSI program. You can get a picture of the type of activity we ran into, like the number of entities that we had to work with—and there were some 1,350 separate entities within the

50 states in the country—all with different types of systems; some with very manualized types of statistical systems, and others with the very most complex computer-type systems to assimilate into our one system in Baltimore, Maryland. The idea was that since SSA already had a computer system that could handle the Title II, program we could expand the computer capacity to also handle easily the SSI program. Again, before we actually got into business on January 1, 1974, we were faced wtih two pieces of legislation which gave us more problems during the planning and negotiation stages. Initially though, our main activity centered around trying to convert all these records that I was mentioning—each document being representative of an individual who was receiving benefits from a state or county. Each record had to be converted to our computer system in Baltimore so that we could make the first payments under the new Federal program by January 1. Congress realized that in the initial legislation, they had not taken into consideration the fact that states had an option or would have an option to supplement the basic benefits or not to supplement it, and this would possibly mean that some states might decide not to give the people that had been receiving a certain payment level as much as they had received in the past. So the one piece of legislation that was passed in July, 1973, required the states to meet what we call mandatory minimum payment levels. This meant the states must pay each individual receiving as of December, 1973, the same amount as of January 1, 1974, thus assuming that there wouldn't be any loss of benefits. We quickly realized the fact that many, many payment variations existed in the country, state by state.

So, we got into a complex system that we had not envisioned getting into initially. Initially, we were thinking of a flat grant payment schedule system. We've departed substantially from that because of the complexity that existed within the country; because of state desires to maintain given payment levels and because of state legislative requirements to maintain payment levels adequate for the populations in those particular states and counties. A good example of the problems we had in trying to work with the states in converting to federal payments as of January 1, 1974, occurred right here in California where the state administration felt that it had established a certain level of payments which was adequate and had administrative rights to put these payments into effect. This was challenged in court by a legal assistance group and the courts found in their favor. This required last minute state legislation. The state legislation was actually passed on December 5, 1973. We had to be in place to make those payments by January 1, 1974. We were actually killing our computer programmers off during that period of time, as you can imagine. We had people working more or less around the clock—actually sleeping at the building. I've heard of a few divorces actually occurring because the husbands weren't available for month after month. But, we did generally make it in many respects, and we got the bulk of the checks out by January 1, 1974 for those people who were converted from the state roles. At least 96 percent of the people converted received their checks as of January 1, which I think would be considered a staggering job. However, from the standpoint of each individual that 4 percent represents, including many people who needed money desperately but we didn't get checks to, it required that the states fill in and make monies available in the interim period. As a result of experience since we got involved with the program many legislative actions are either being taken or are being looked at, at this point in time. Recommendations for change are being made regularly. As was mentioned earlier this morning, I met with the Senate Finance Committee representatives just last week to review what's actually happening in the SSI program with the idea of making necessary changes to make this program work more smoothly. Also, I might say this personally: that having worked in an organization like Social Security where we are involved with administering a program or programs that Congress legislates, I can see changes that are necessary come about through a number of methods. But changes appropriate to particular groups, especially minority groups, have to come through consolidated effort and through our legislators to achieve solid results. It's very evident, working within that the pressures from particular areas can have effect in moving directions of given programs to where they should be, and cause them to take into consideration the needs of a given population or group.

Again, the philosophy behind the SSI program was to provide a semblance of dignity and a benefit level appropriate to help maintain the individual in some basic capacity; and that's why it's called Supplemental Security Income. It's not meant to support the individual completely. It is meant as a supplement, and that's all it can be in the way that Congress passed the present law. As some of you may have heard, and it was mentioned to me earlier this morning, Secretary Weinberger and others have been talking recently about a positive or negative income tax approach towards income maintenance. This may be a better kind of approach towards solving the problem areas that we're facing as far as people in need in our country are concerned. I can't particularly say, but it may be a better way than the present programs we are administering. We do definitely need to remove some of the complexities involved with the SSI program, and this can only be accomplished by outside pressures, legislative approaches, and sometimes recommendations from within the Social Security Administation.

In order to provide this dignity I was talking about or a lack of stigma as far as welfare is concerned, Congress decided that Social Security for another reason was an appropriate agency to have administer this program in that we presently have some 1,300 installations nationwide called branch offices, district offices, and teleservice centers. We are in business to administer the Social Security provisions, primarily Title II, up until the time of the SSI enactment. By utilizing the same facilities and the same staff and utilizing the same approach that was used in the past regarding Title II benefits, it was felt that the individuals would receive all the services necessary to assure that they receive their benefits on time or an adequate explanation of the requirements for receiving such benefits. The philosophy of SSI was somewhat of a departure from the basic philosophy of the Title II program since Title II is an earned-right program. That was the kind of public relations jargon that had been used for years when talking to the public. So we had to curtail the Title II type of public relations approach and still provide the same basic interview and claims development techniques; the same basic courtesy was to be afforded the individual when he came into the office and wanted either Title II or SSI benefits—in some cases, both benefits.

I'd like to quote a few statistics that might be of interest to you regarding how much effect the SSI program actually has as far as money and numbers of people are concerned. For example, comparing December of 1973 and March of 1975, the most recent statistics we have: in Arizona, we had as aged recipients under the SSI program 12,760 people. In March 1975, in Arizona, that statistic went up to 14,196 people. In California, our largest state in this region, aged recipients alone numbered 285,827 in 1973. In March of 1975, that statistic went up to 324,267. In Hawaii, the 1973 figure was 3,213 aged recipients; in March 1975, that went up to 5,167. For the four state, San Francisco region, the aged recipients in 1973 were 303,000; in March 1975, that went up to 347,000. Also, as far as total recipients in all categories—that's all aged, blind, and disabled combined—the California figure for 1973 was 518,000, and for March of 1975 that went up to 620,000 for all categories. And nationally, the total figure in December of 1973 was 3,135,736. That went up approximately one million by March 1975 so that we're now paying 4,124,703 people.

As far as money is concerned—which is probably of more interest—in California each month we're presently paying some $98,693,000 for all categories. Out of that 98 million dollars, 57 million dollars is state money and 41 million dollars is federal money. So that tells you why the State of California is quite concerned about every issue regarding the SSI program: because of the staggering amount of money that it means to the state as far as state dollars for state supplements. The supplements are actually handled through a bookkeeping transaction with the Social Security Administration. For example, in California a check covering Supplemental Payments is actually sent to us each month so that we can make a single payment which includes the federal benefit and the State Supplement for each eligible individual. Nationally, the total amount of SSI payment for March 1974 was $469,410,000. So you can see, of the total for the whole country for all categories, of 469 million, 98 million was being paid in California, which reflects the size of the recipient population and the amount of money being paid in just one state. The complexities go along with that size because of varying approaches by state legislators, a shift of conservative to liberal administrations, especially in California, which we expect will bring some change to benefit the individual. However, we know that it's going to come more slowly because of the limitations of money available. Those limitations are very, very evident and being made more evident to us each time we have to discuss money issues with the state.

RESEARCH AND ITS RELATION TO POLICY FORMULATION

Dr. Sharon Moriwaki, Professor
Ethel Percy Andrus Gerontology Center
University of Southern California

I suppose I'm a ′damper′ here when so many people are doing such impressive things, but I think with its requisite of careful examination of what we have done, what we should do, and what we are doing, research is very important. I know that in the past Institutes, we've had some lively discussions between practitioners and researchers, and it seems that ″never the twain shall meet″. But, we hope that in the workshop today, we might be able to resolve some of this and see that we are trying to go in somewhat the same direction. In terms of looking at the relationship between policy formation and research, when you look at any kind of relationship you really have to look at the variables of policy, formation and research.

In terms of policy, I've heard distinguished speakers about everything happening on federal, state, and local levels and have come away from that realizing there is no policy, there is no national policy. We tend to be diverse; different geographical areas, different ethnic groups, different class groupings. We say we're individuals—we're different and yet we try to develop a policy where we go across the board and deal with everyone the same way. Perhaps we should start speaking of different classifications for policy, lower level policy perhaps, more flexible policy for the specialized groups such as the minority elderly. In terms of policy, again I think that it seems to be quite random, that it goes in a direction until there are negative repercussions. It seems to be quite well stated in what Kissinger said about the Cambodian invasion: "Admit you're right, it's bound to happen statistically sometime," and it seems this is the way we work with policy, we keep going until we find out we're wrong. And yet to me, policy requires that you set guidelines, that you create a map. Planning—the big word today is planning. And what does that mean? I think that if we want to create a map of where we want to go, we've got to know where we want to go. We've got to get goals and priorities. And I think it's really important to also know where we are, and I think that's where research can come in. What I'd like to do in the workshop would be to discuss some of these issues, to see what is really conflictual in some of these policies.

We say the goal is independent, dignified living, reduced isolation, whatever, for the elderly. How is that happening in the federal, state and local levels? The implementation is important, but we also have to have lower level kinds of objectives to know that we're actually going in that direction. You start examining what individual, independent, dignified, living is, and you realize that it's a lot of different things to a lot of different people. I think that the most important kind of contribution research can make is to really get some adequate accurate data of where we are. We're such a technologically advanced society in that somehow we don't know how many people we really have, nor do we know what they're really like. It's just that when you're thinking of planning, and everyone's talking about planning; we're basing it on the little statistics we do have. And that's scratching the surface. We know that the elderly are disadvantaged, that they have lower incomes, that their health is failing, that they should have some kind of health plan. But we haven't really looked at the quality of the kinds of services they do receive. We're not looking at what it means to them. I think here at San Diego State a study on ethnic minorities might be a great contribution in that respect. When you do interview different minority elderly, you should take into consideration their backgrounds. We talk about cultural background, minority status, and yet when interviewers go out into the community—and this is a big rip-off of researchers going into the community and exploiting them—that they're not taking into consideration some of the norms, some of the cultural values that these people have and treating them as people. I think the movie that we saw yesterday brings into focus this need for looking at a longitudinal history of the individual and who you're dealing with. And in terms of planning, in terms of national policy, we would have to use statistics, we would have have to use some kind of norm average which really blocks out a lot of the individual differences. OK, as Frank says, Perhaps we all have the same needs. We all just need food, clothing, shelter. But, the way in which they are is also important. You can give someone a house or a roof over his head—it could be a highrise condominium yet it doesn't make him comfortable. He's not familiar; he wants to be close to the land. These are the kinds of considerations I think should be made, and we should find out what people want. Now in terms of research, I see it taking various forms. One is purely descriptive, looking at the needs and assessing the needs of the people, with the idea that we should probably start a little bit further back to look at some of the middle-aged to see if there is uniformity in aging, and if certain needs do come just with aging.

Also, I think in terms of policy formation when we do have a policy, we should also look in terms of evaluation. All of us are doers. We're all doing and we don't have the time to think about what we're doing, yet I think it's important; that's where evaluation comes in. Knowing where you want to go, saying OK, these are the objectives I have, this is where I want to get, and to evaluate the programs to see if they are getting where they should be going. If they aren't, scrap them. I think you've got to start trying to see if there are any kinds of uniformity in terms of what works. We seem to be a society that's really directionless; if you look at the television programs, they are a reflection of society. They seem to be—well, one program works. Like Archie Bunker works. Then the Jeffersons come on. Then the Hot'l Baltimore. I mean they're all the same format. There's no creativity; no trying to find whether something else might work better with less cost. You can at least get information together so that you can disseminate it, so you can say something works or something doesn't work, so that we don't have all this duplication with things that don't work.

I also would like to look at perhaps researching the process of impact; how we're all talking about how to impact legislators, how to impact executive administrators; and yet no one knows how to do it. I think some of that has come out in some of the panel speaker presentations in terms of knowing the individual, working with an individual legislator. And I think its also important that we do have to deal with people up there; perhaps this is part of the process. At University of Southern California Gerontology Center a National Science Foundation funded project directed by Dr. Bengston is doing sort of this kind of thing. They're interviewing policy-makers and professionals and consumers to determine the discrepancies in terms of priorities, needs, and process. I think this is important—it might be a very good contribution to the field. I think more of this has to be done by people who are working the field, who have had the experience, so that their approach can be disseminated through other people. I guess the most important thing I would like to say in terms of impacting is that you should know who your congressmen are, that you should find out who your state legislators are, that also there are digests, like the Congressional Digest. The state puts out a little brochure describing each legislator, with a description of what his constituents are like. Now that's important in terms of minority elderly. If you have a senator or representative who is in a highly black, or a highly elderly area, you should contact those legislators because this is how you would impact. These would be the people who would be willing to do something about certain issues dealing with elderly minorities.

Stan Nielson
Acting Director
California Office on Aging

To begin with, it would be significant to state that in the first draft of our new state plan—
the one that's now being drafted for next year (1976)—the first priority listed is to improve
the quality of life for the poor and the minorities. This is a matter of administrative choice
that happens to coincide with the federal perspective. We are receiving some considerable
encouragement from the federal government to go in this direction, but if that were not the
case, we would be quite prepared to take the federal government on, and this is the policy.
I think it's significant, though, to recognize that we are receiving some very clear federal
direction in this regard. I think it's perhaps significant to bear in mind that Commissioner
Fleming, the Commissioner of Aging, is also the Commissioner of Civil Rights. And that is,
I think, very significant. I think that gives us considerable power when we're trying to do
anything that's going to improve the lifestyles or the functioning of minority elderly because
we have combined at the federal level, in the office of one man, a person who is concerned
with both of these programs. I think that's a point that we might well bear in mind.

Now in terms of legislation for the state, I think that the notion of inviting suggestions to the
the State Office on Aging about where we might be going would be particularly significant
in the field of legislation. I think you can recognize that the current administration has
discovered that there is a severe financial problem in California. There is both a reluctance
to accept the notion that all problems can be solved with money, and a keen awareness of
the fact that there is not enough money to solve all the problems. Now I think those are
two very significant points, and they have considerable impact upon the administration's
policies toward legislation in general, and, certainly, in the social areas where the need for
funds is so great. What this means is that this year the likelihood of the California administration supporting very expensive legislative programs to solve social ills, including the field
of aging, would not be good. I think what this means is first of all that we're expected to
make better use of resources we now have. And, I'm quite in sympathy with that notion.
It's really from my perspective painfully obvious that there are many things that we could
do to improve the administration of services to the elderly and to the minority poor. In
doing that, I think we can then prepare to get our house in order so that we can go in good
faith to the governor, or to the legislature, and say we're now being efficient and effective
in the delivery of services to the elderly poor and minority. Now we have identified the
priority needs and have identified the real opportunities for program services that will be
of great benefit to the elderly. And perhaps they are going to be sufficiently cost-beneficial
that they will actually result in no increased expenditures for the State.

I see the current emphasis being on improving what we have and being sure the services are
really reaching the individuals for whom they are intended. Let me give you an example of
what I mean by that. I'm thinking of one nutrition site located directly in the heart of a
fairly high concentration of minorities Principally these are black people. But in visiting
the nutrition site, you see very few black faces. I think that's a problem. I have no problem
with the location of the nutrition project except with the specific place chosen. It's right in
the center of the area, but it's really not accessible which means you have to have a car,
which means that we're in that site only serving the people who are already fairly comfortable. In that case, they tend not to be the minority and not to be the poor. In other words,
we're doing a miserable job there. It's a beautiful site, food is good and they have arts and

crafts. It's almost an ideal site in every respect except for the fact that we're not being effective; we're not reaching the people we are supposed to reach. I think that's tragic. Our first priority in the future is to be sure that we make services available to those who really need them and to be sure that we are not wasteful.

In the field of aging, with resources so limited and the need so great, I think we have to recognize that any inefficiency we allow to continue means that someone is going to go hungry, someone is going to go without medical services, or transportation services, or appropriate housing, or other necessary services. We just can't afford to have inefficiency or ineffectiveness. I think that needs to be the general thrust of our concern at the state level in the field of aging for the next several months. But after that, after having put our house in order, we need to have a fairly significant legislative thrust emphasizing, first of all, those programs which will have considerable payoff not only in terms of individual benefit, but also in terms of being able to improve the total delivery system. I would like us to be thinking about what are the first needs, because again I'm acutely aware of the fact that our resources are so limited in relationship to the needs and that we're only going to be able to do the very most important things. So let's be sure we know what the most important things are.

I like to think first of all—employment. Some of you may list something else first, but I think employment is very important because if those who are able to work and want to work, have an opportunity, they can take care of any of their other problems—transportation, housing, access to a neighborhood that is more appropriate or desirable. They have more mobility and they have more freedom. Literally, economic power means freedom in many of the other areas. And so to me, employment is a very important opportunity.

Closely associated with employment is education because we find that in the field of aging, age itself is not so debilitating or disabling as the fact that you are elderly, a member of a minority, and undereducated. I hope you've all had a chance to refer to the recent Harris Poll which points out that youth looks upon old age as a period of an unpleasant experience in life and that this "unpleasant experience" is intensified by undereducation and by race. If you happen to be a minority, you're faced with the kinds of problems that indeed place you in double jeopardy. The notion of double jeopardy I think is worth spending just a few moments on because it implies the need for social action and, perhaps in many cases, legislative change. Some of these problems can be dealt with to some extent by administrative action, but I'm sure some of them are going to require some legislative support. Statistically, minorities are behind in average length of life, income, use of health services and mobility. The notion of mobility not only influences our life opportunities but also our image of ourselves and our life enrichment.

I think it's significant to recognize that money is power, not only purchasing power, but it produces freedom—freedom of choice and freedom of mobility. I think it's significant to bear in mind that whites are considerably more likely to have savings when they reach the golden years than minorities are, therefore being freer. I think it's significant to bear in mind that they're more likely to own their home than minorities. All of these factors indicate that minorities are placed in double jeopardy when they are fortunate enough to live to the golden years. As we encourage the development of Area Agencies on aging, in local community involvement programs, I think we can be sure that if we are alert to the opportunity to place first things first, that the needs of the poor are at the top, minority needs will go right with them. And for that reason, as we're stating objectives in the State Office on Aging, we use the two terms in the same clause, poor and minority, because there is such a close correlation.

It is the responsibility of the Area Agency on Aging to identify the needs of the minority poor in their area. I think it's important for leaders in the community in the field of aging to be aware of this and to be sure that minorities appear at public hearings for the development and approval of local plans for Area Agencies and to see that area plans serve as the primary area of input for the State Office on Aging for needs identification. If a poor job is done at a community level of identifying and prioritizing the needs, then that means that we are going to have limited access at the state level. Funding decisions are made on the basis of how many elderly poor there are, and if we don't know how many elderly poor there are, then the funds are going to go somewhere else and that means that the allocations will not meet the real needs. We don't know well enough even where the minority poor are, and we don't know what their needs are. Census information in respect to minorities is difficult to interpret. Sure we have the official statistics, we have the official reports, we have all of the same techniques that any other governmental agency has access to in identifying the needs. But, the point is, that's not enough because the needs change and because the needs even at the point of report frequently are not accurate or incomplete, and I don't think we're going to have the true complete story unless we have a lot of input from a lot of people writing to addresses like this, contacting your local board of supervisors, your local city council, your local area agency on aging, to be sure that that kind of input is made at the local level and therefore reflected in local reports to the state level.

Mandatory retirement on the basis of age is one of the greatest social evils facing us. I think it's almost incomprehensible that it is not only legal, but constitutional to force someone into mandatory retirement and, in all too many cases, into forced poverty just because one day he is older than he was another day. Now a person may be at the top of the ladder in an organization one day and the next day he's literally unemployable anywhere. For many people, mandatory retirement means mandatory poverty. Going back to the Harris Poll, it's kind of significant to bear in mind that the preponderance of people surveyed felt that if someone is forced into mandatory retirement, it is then the government's resonsibility to be sure that they have an adequate income. That's not now the case. There are many people who are not able to work, who are not allowed to work, who are not permitted to by law; and when I say not permitted to by law, I mean that the Supreme Court has interpreted as constitutional mandatory retirement. That means, therefore, they are forced into retirement by law in my terms. What is the opportunity for those people? How can you imagine a more hopeless situation than knowing that you can't get a job, that you don't have any money, and you don't have any income? What kind of hope is there for an older person forced into retirement? Well, let me just say this, that the State Office on Aging is taking a very vigorous stand on this. We believe firmly that it ought to be eliminated and we would be very, very willing to be the first state agency to have waived any mandatory retirement provisions. I am quite convinced that if we're given that privilege that other departments will find it to their advantage to join us and before long break down the age barriers.

Funding and the Area Agency on Aging. The Area on Aging concept is a compromise between the legislative concern for enormous unmet needs, in the field of aging, and very limited resources. And so the Area Agency on Aging, to some extent, I think, has been developed as a mechanism to absorb some of the community concern for the need for services without great financial investment. The basic notion is that no matter how much money we spend there is not enough in the Treasury to meet all the needs of the elderly, nor should there be. The elderly want to meet many of their own needs. They don't want to have services shelled out continually. So the point is that the resources are critically limited. The notion of the multiplier effect comes in also: if we can pool and coordinate resources, we can reach out and tap services that are already being made available in the community but that the elderly are not receiving. If we can do that, in effect, we can multiply the dollars made available to the Area Agency on Aging without it actually directly funding a whole series of projects. There are many Area Agencies throughout the country that fund projects directly only once. They make a decision once, such as a transportation program, for example, and there are no other programs funded from then on. It's just a matter of continuing that decision, and that could well be the way that some Area Agencies would go. So the point here is that the Area Agency on Aging does not have resources to become the major funding source for social programs for minority poor elderly. It has a little bit, it can do a little bit, but its primary function is to serve as a focal point of awareness in the community to plug into existing resources and to multiply those resources and to encourage the generation of new services where possible.

The Area Agency on Aging has to be skillful at persuasion, imaginative, creative at discovery, in recognizing how to reach out into the community and take advantage of services that other people are already using. It has to reach out in the community and convince businesses that they ought to be involved, to reach out and convince insurance companies that it's to their advantage to encourage nutritional and health services for the elderly, because it prolongs their lives and therefore delays the time when the insurance company must pay premiums. You know, these are really some pretty high skills, and they are based on the assumption that if the Area Agency does a good job that it will indeed have this multiplier effect. Now, by a good job, I don't mean the direct provision of services. That's not what the business of the Area Agency on Aging is all about. The business of the Area Agency on Aging is pooling and coordination. It's multiplying availability of services through its function. Now, if you see that as administration and therefore as waste, then you're challenging the basic concept of the Area Agency and that's fine, go ahead and do that. But at the same time, you can't criticize the conduct of the Area Agency on Aging for doing that because that's its charge and it cannot have its funds unless it carries out that charge. The state cannot receive its funds unless it does the same. Now, if you don't like that approach, you need a federal resolution through federal legislation. But I would suggest that before you try that kind of change, that you give it a chance to work. It's a new process. The area agencies are new and if we're talking about this kind of skill level that's required, we're talking about reaching out in a community, plugging in, and developing new resources and new programs. I hope as I am saying that, you're thinking of time to develop resources, time to develop programs, time to plug into existing services. It takes time to pool, it takes time to coordinate, and the Area Agency on Aging has not had time to demonstrate whether it is going to work. I say that we have a big commitment to it. Give it some time to work, don't expect it to have immediate results right now and don't expect its results now to be increased in provision of services, because that's not what it is designed to do.

The role of the federal government. I think significant improvements and significantly greater levels of funding are quite possible, but I think we find considerable conflict between Congress and the President. One of the great conflicts that has been going on in the last several months has been on Title VII funds. The Congress has appropriated over 50 million dollars in extra funds for Title VII. That's a 50 percent increase, and the administration could have released those funds a long time ago. They have just barely released it, and we've had several conflicting bits of information about when it can be used and how it will be used. It's been very, very clear that the federal administration has not been interested in making that money available; and it's been because of congressional pressure that it has been made available. Now, because of that, I think we have to recognize that the Congress is indeed responsive, and I think that gives you some clues as to where you can go to be sure that other worthy programs are considered and funded. There are several legislators in Congress and in the state who have been very, very effective in carrying forward the programs of the elderly.

Ultimately, the money for services comes from the people and therefore, I think the point about being sure of what it is the people want and need is really the major concern. We have

44   to get back to that. I don't really feel that you can ever say we've identified the needs because I believe it's a living process, it's an ongoing, continuous process, and if we feel we've ever defined them and we don't need to consider them any further, then I think we have established a bureaucracy of power in office rather than power in the people. I think the power must be with the people, and our concern is the power being with the elderly. One of the greatest areas of power is not just their ability for influence, but the ability of the elderly for service. We're where we are because of the elderly literally, and I'm keenly aware of that. I'm very much aware of the contributions of those who've gone before me— my relatives and those who are not related to me. But, I think we ought to be emphasizing the great potential that the elderly have for service; one of the biggest things that concerns me is the waste of people. I know no greater waste of people than this monumental waste of the edlerly.

The flavor that I'd like to see us leave on is the notion that we have a very big problem and we're not going to solve all the problems overnight. They didn't occur overnight; they've been with us for many decades and many of them have been with us for hundreds of years. But that doesn't mean that we need to be complacent about them or that we need to accept them. It means that we need to be challenging, that we need to be unhappy with the conditions that exist and that we need to find ways to overcome the kind of system of delivery and nondelivery of services. We need to find ways of turning a problem, a dilemma, into an opportunity for improvement. We need to find a way to recognize that poison that we see in a problem as a gold nugget, as an opportunity for improvement in services. I think we can do that only if we have a kind of openness, a kind of trust that I had thought we had had and that I welcomed.

There's so much that needs to be done in the field of aging, and there is an opportunity for everybody to make a contribution. There's no need for anybody to feel the need to pull position for power or position for an opportunity to be heard. Instead, I feel we need to look upon aging as an area where we do need greater emphasis on morality and on ethics. I also think we probably have never been in a time where there is such an opportunity for social change as there is in the field of aging now where the eldely can be improved, where they can have opportunities in the various areas of need that have for so long plagued them.

POLITICAL STRATEGIES
AND CONSIDERATIONS

POLITICAL CONSIDERATIONS FOR CHANGE

Ruben Dominguez, Director
Department of Human Resources
San Diego, California

If this conference is going like most conferences, you have heard that what we need is a comprehensive plan on aging at the federal, state and local levels. You have heard very special interest groups—from the Chicanos to the Pan Asians to the Blacks—say that we need some strategies as we deal with the problems of special groups in aging. You have also heard undoubtedly that counties and cities are not sensitive to the needs of the aging. The tragic thing about this is that it is all correct, and that the only way we are going to deal with it is in the arena of politics. With that in mind, I would like to make some comments in relationship to some specific strategies that could be utilized in dealing with this area.

First of all, I think we should all be aware, as we undoubtedly are, that the whole notion of shifting certain kinds of funding from categorical funding to block grants—with particular emphasis on Revenue Sharing or special Revenue Sharing—has some implications for local government and state government. One of the implications is that whether it is local government or whether it is state government we really don't have the capacity at this time to respond comprehensively to these problems. We have been trained and we know how to operate and that's the reason why many times we respond and say we need a dial-a-bus program; so we fund it until the funding runs out. Then we have a big battle on that, and then there's a battle within that arena. We need a nutrition program; so we fund a nutrition program, and there's a big battle on that. And the funding is getting close to the end, and then we deal with that. So, when we say we don't have comprehensive plans and real social policies, I think this is true across the board, whether dealing with the problems of children, youth, senior citizens, or older Americans, or whatever the nomenclature happens to be at that time.

I think, though, in dealing with these realities, one of the essential aspects of it is the attempt to understand where the pressure points are, who has the power at any given time. It is not enough, for example, to say that what I am going to do is say we need more money for nutrition. While that may be a viable strategy, unless you deal with the power of bureaucracy and the power of the regulations that bureaucracy releases, we won't get effective legislation implemented. The same thing is true in deciding whether or not to put the pressure on the state legislature. But unless we deal with the Office on Aging and their particular problem, we are not really going to solve the basic problem or even begin to release the dollars that are right now sitting in Sacramento unspent. We are aware, for example, that there is anywhere from five to six million dollars available right now not being utilized simply because the organizational structure of the state has been unable to deliver these dollars to the local government. Then, on the other hand, the local government has been floundering around with various political strategies and various political idiosyncracies that leave the people wondering whether our local legislative bodies are not circuses.

I think what we're really saying is that we need to identify the power of the legislative bodies and the elected officials, but we also need to identify the power of the technocrats in the bureaucracies, and to be able to deal with both.

On the local level, it is essential that we keep our communications open with members of the boards of supervisors and city councils, but it is also essential that we keep the channels open with the people in the bureaucracies and particular administrative bodies.

I guess what we are saying is that power and influence is confused and very complex in an urban society, and whether you are talking about senior citizens or older Americans or whatever, it is just a constant search for us to find out where we can turn that pressure point to see that the right thing we believe in happens. It is not enough to say we are in the business of doing good. A lot of people are doing good, but it is the difficulty in understanding all of the complexities that makes it so frustrating for the people who are presently residing in such places like the Golden West Hotel, the Maryland Hotel, and those kinds of center city housing that are really an indictment of our society. There is an inability to distribute our resources in such a way that we reward people not on the basis of their productivity, but in relationship to their needs.

These are the kinds of things you are kicking around, but as you go back into the communities and deal with the local problems, it really is a basic political issue. And it's the kind of pressure and power that we must deal with not only in the elected officials but also within the various administrative structures, because power is just a fuse in those areas. As we look look at a community even like our own we find a big county government that has a preliminary budget of 468 million dollars. We see a city which is approximately the eleventh largest in the country with a preliminary budget of around 213 million dollars. We see thirteen municipalities; we see over a hundred special districts, all with taxing powers. All have an appropriate role in a comprehensive strategy dealing with the problems of older Americans, and it's a very frustrating situation to try to figure out where to go. Many times what occurs is that a suggestion is made on a very narrow basis. When the San Diego Gas and Electric Company suggests that we ought to have utility stamps for senior citizens, it's just another example of how we respond on a very fragmented basis. From where I sit the last thing that the Department of Public Welfare needs is another categorical program with another set of eligibility determinations, with additional administrative costs to determine who is going to be eligible for those utility stamps. Right now in the Department of Public Welfare it costs us one dollar to distribute three. That's shameful. With the same reality, we know that we are going to continue to expend all these dollars in determining who is eligible, because we are right now doing a survey of all the forms that we have in the state in the Welfare Department. Our last count in the state alone is 196 forms. This is a problem, and it isn't because the people don't want to do good. It's because we have responded to our legislative bodies. It is an attempt to begin a massive reform.

What we actually need in the last analysis is more dollars in people's pockets to be distributed in a better way. And then when we do that, we can clearly separate income maintenance from services and not continue to sell services as a method of solving poverty but as a very necessary activity in the society. I would not be in a position to argue against the validity of a homemaker program that goes into a home and helps senior citizens maintain their independence. I would not be in a position to argue that we should not do something about child abuse. What we need is a better strategy in convincing our legislative bodies that we need more comprehensiveness in dealing with human problems.

Julian C. Dixon
Assembly, 49th District
Los Angeles, California

"To discuss old age in euphemistic terms trivializes it. There is nothing wrong with getting old."

So said Margaret Kuhn, one of the founders of the Gray Panthers, in a recent interview.

The Gray Panthers are devoted to fighting ageism—not age—but ageism, as in myths, fallacies and outright discrimination.

In thinking about this conference with the title of "Institute on Minority Aging," it occurred to me that the aging are truly a minority, and the special problems of the minority aging cannot necessarily be answered by legislation. The overlying problem is one of economics—money—as it is the problem in so many other areas.

The aging, as a minority group of its own, is growing. The Census of 1900 classified one out of every 25 persons as in the aging category. In the Census in 1970, one out of every ten Americans were aged. Projections to the future, provided the birth rate continues to decline, anticipate that those 65 years of age and over will constitute well over 10 percent of the total population.

Minorities are reflected in the 1970 census in interesting ways. For instance, figures show that 32 percent of the black population in the country exists on an income below the poverty level or low income level. Another example is that only 57 percent of the elderly in the non-English ethnic minority groups speak English.

We must also keep in mind that the minority aged have not only their own special problems, but in addition have the same problems in common with the "majority" aging.

The word "problem" itself is derived from a Latin word meaning "something thrown forward." In fact, one of the English definitions of problem is "a question raised for inquiry, consideration or solution—an intricate unsettled question. Nowhere does it say "impossible to solve" or "unsettleable."

I found it particularly interesting that a recent Harris Poll taken for the National Council of the Aging showed that for every older person who felt that his or her own life was worse now than he or she thought it would be, there were three who said that life is better now than they expected. Even more enlightening was the fact that four out of five older people said that they could look back on their past lives with satisfaction, and three in four felt that their present is as interesting as it ever was. Over half were making plans for their future.

So the aged themselves do not find their problems unsolvable. Neither should the rest of us. And, especially, neither should the elected officials of the state and country.

As Chairman of the Assembly Public Employees and Retirement Committee, I have a special interest in the financial independence aspect of the aged. In that same Harris Poll, it was noted that an overwhelming majority of Americans of all ages said that the government has a duty to provide for older people at a level allowing them to live comfortably. And I agree with that majority.

But in order to attain financial independence, the aged must have brought in an adequate salary during their fully-employed years to allow for that independence. Normally, the unemployed are thought of as being young, unskilled and quite often members of one of California's minority groups. Taking into consideration that the aged *are* a minority group, there is much truth in this observation. Because of experience and reliability, the older worker is often in a good position to retain his job. Once displaced or unemployed, however, the prospect of re-employment for the older worker is uncertain. This phenomenon becomes progressively worse the older he becomes. Among those who lose their jobs, the average duration of unemployment is significantly longer for the older workers.

Age discrimination is an ever-present factor for the older worker. One out of every two jobs in which there are openings is closed to all persons over 65, and one out of four jobs to persons over 45. At the turn of the last century, about two-thirds of the elderly men were still employed. In 1970, only one-fourth of the men in the same age group were employed. This means that more and more older people are retiring or being forced to retire at an earlier age.

RETIREMENT

Legislation has been introduced to provide important employment options for those older persons who would want to continue working. For those who don't, after retirement, on the average, income drops over 50 percent. Large savings accounts, kept up for years, are made less valuable because of inflation and serious illness. Ninety percent of the older couples receive retirement benefits. These are much less than the total income earned during the latter years of work and in most cases, only 30 to 40 percent. Consequently, it is easy to understand that older people live near the poverty level even if we have never witnessed it personally.

Despite horrific figures of untimely deaths shortly after retirement, in itself, it is probably not the villain causing lowered health and energy. When analyzed, figures show that about 50 percent retire because of poor health and therefore are already vulnerable to disease and death. The other 50 percent not only have no higher or earlier death rates than actuarial figures indicate, but also many of them enjoy *improved* health.

Recent research by the National Institute of Mental Health points to the fact that many persons tend to retire gradually.

PENSION PLANS

The key to "successful" retirement is a pension plan. In California, 60 percent of the workers are covered by private pension plans. For those in private employment, this comes to about 3 1/2 million workers. Despite this impressive record, there are some 2 million California residents who are not covered by private pension plans and will probably never receive pension benefits. This group is a diverse one and includes individuals from many different income levels. A substantial majority, however, come from lower income backgrounds—agricultural workers, marginal business operations, and the self-employed.

Incentives for saving money for retirement are few, even if they could afford to do so, for people with very low paying jobs. But both the federal and state government *do* provide tax incentives for contributors to pension plans.

There are three ways in which the federal government treats pension plans through taxes:

1. **Qualified Pension Plans**—These must meet special funding coverage and anti-discrimination requirements for qualification under the Federal Internal Revenue Code (Section 401). This entitles a plan to a unique combination of tax results.

2. **Non-Qualified Plans**—These are plans which have *not* complied with the coverage and anti-discrimination requirements for qualified plans. These plans receive less favorable tax treatment.

3. **Plans for the Self-Employed**—Some of the tax benefits of qualified plans are extended to pension programs for self-employed persons. Most of the federal provisions for self-employed pension plans have been incorporated into state law.

The Public Employees and Retirement Committee in the Assembly alone has had 183 bills pass before it to date this year, and its counterpart in the Senate has had approximately 200. Of those, none are substantially directed toward private pension plans. The reasons for this is that federal law has pre-empted states from regulating private pension plans except in very minor areas.

PRIVATE PENSION PLANS

Private pension plans have become a nationwide concern due to questionable practices regarding disclosure, administration and trustee conduct.

In November of 1973, a Preliminary Report by the Chairman of the Senate Committee on Business and Professions on the Operation of Private Pension Plans listed a summary of findings relating to private pension plans. At the end of this list was the following statement:

> *Based on preliminary findings of the Chairman of the Senate Committee on Business and Professions, summarized by this report, there exists an urgent need for thorough and comprehensive state regulatory authority covering the operation of private pension plans in order to assure that plan participants are treated in a fair and equitable manner and to assure plan participants that funds set aside for future benefits are invested and handled in a manner which will guarantee future benefits.*

Consequently, during the 1973-74 session, the State Legislature spent a considerable amount of time attempting to formulate legislation that would regulate private pension plans. Included in the major bill introduced during the session were provisions insuring that retirement rights would be vested within a specific period of time, that all plans were written in such a manner that an average individual could understand them, that all plans were properly funded so no individaul would lose benefits were a company to go bankrupt, and that all plans would be properly administered.

However, before the legislation introduced at the state level became law, the federal government enacted the Employee Retirement Income Security Act of 1974, which not only regulates private pension plans in this country but preempts state governments from regulating such plans through state laws.

So, although the state has no direct control over private pension plans, I feel it does have the obligation to see how the federal government is accomplishing this monumental task of pension reform and to see that the people of California do not get lost in a nationwide bureaucratic shuffle.

It is too early at this point to ascertain just how successful the federal pension reform bill will be, but the state will carefully watch what happens and possibly counter any negative outcomes of that plan.

PUBLIC EMPLOYEES AND RETIREMENT COMMITTEE AND PENSION PLANS

That, then, brings us to public employee retirement plans over which the state *does* have direct control.

Although the Public Employees and Retirement Committee is a policy committee, which means it considers the subject matter a piece of legislation as opposed to the fiscal impact, its every act has a *direct fiscal impact* on the state budget. It passes judgement on which bills will or won't be effective or which will be more effective than others.

Most bills that pass through this committee can be justified on policy. The committee can justify passing out any bill which improves the lot of any public employee group of people. But once out of this committee, those bills still must be dealt with on a money basis.

The other members of the committee and I realize that people living on a fixed income need help, but the state does not have the resources or the economic stability to help all people at once. So, some bills will pass out of the committee this year, and some won't; some will pass out next year, and some won't. Some will and some won't go to the Senate, and even fewer will be passed on to the Governor to be signed into law.

This year, the number-one priority relative to public retirement plans is **cost-of-living increases**.

As you may be aware, the yearly cost-of-living increase provided retired members of the Public Employees Retirement System and the State Teachers' Retirement System is 2 percent maximum. Obviously, the actual cost-of-living increase being experienced each year far exceeds that. This raises the question, Why not pay the actual cost-of-living rather than a maximum of 2 percent?

The answer is simply that of availability of funds. For instance, for each 1 percent increase in the Public Employees Retirement System cost-of-living factor, the cost to the state would approximate 60 to 65 million dollars per year, either from the local or the state taxpayer. For each 1 percent in the State Teachers Retirement System cost-of-living factor, the cost to the state or school districts would approximate 54 million dollars per year.

CONCLUSION

All of this indicates that the legislators are concerned with public and private pensions. At this time, the matter is in the hands of the federal government and we are urging and watching Congress.

But where we have the power, the authority, we are acting. Basically, that is two areas: Public employees and teachers. These are important also, because the proposals which pass through our committee affect up to one million people in this state. This sets an example for and creates pressure on private industry to act in a like manner in providing suitable retirement benefits for all working men and women.

Only by promoting good retirement benefits for all people can we attain good benefits for minority people.

Peter Chacon
Assemblyman, 79th District
San Diego, California
Presented by Stuart Queen

Difficult as it is for most people to live their senior years in reasonable physical comfort and psychological health, it is most difficult and challenging to the aging minority person, who, through no fault of his own, never acquired access at a young age to the Social Security System which would have allowed him to reap at least some basic benefits in old age. How can you expect a person to receive a fat pension or to acquire a life savings or to get a decent social security check at 70 years of age when he could not get a decent weekly check working ten hours a day, at 30 years of age in a menial job which wasn't covered by any benefits.

You, the professional gerontologist, practitioner, and student, are familiar with formal data, the facts and figures, better than I. But, it has been brought home to me personally by the people who live in my district.

I appreciate the effort of the Center on Aging, and I recognize the need for this Institute on Minority Aging. If our society has not begun to deal adequately with the majority aging, it's a foregone conclusion that the minority aging are not getting their fair share of attention or action from government.

The recent Harris Survey, commissioned by the National Council on Aging, indicates that the public favors government support of retired persons.

Those who choose to retire or who are no longer able to continue their work should have the right to retire, the public feels, and to turn to the government for financial support. Asked, "Who should provide income for older people when they are no longer working?" Sixty-five percent of those responding to the Harris Poll said the Federal Government should, through Social Security.

Further findings underscore the idea that the government, with its powers of taxation, has the responsibility and means to support older people (18 percent to 14 percent). Those under 65 agree even more strongly than the retired people themselves.

The total public (76 percent to 19 percent) also feels that "No matter how much (or little) a person earned during his working years, he should be able to have enough money to live on comfortably when he is older and retired."

Agreeing almost unanimously that older people have the right to live comfortably, the public also endorsed support of older people in line with rising prices, recognizing that persons on fixed incomes may be victimized most by inflation. By an overwhelming majority (97 percent), the public, both old and young, supported cost-of-living escalators in Social Security payments.

My special role today is to exchange with you some ideas on how we can affect state legislation so that some priority is a given to those on the absolute bottom—the older minority persons.

I have no secret formula—no cure at all—no grandiose strategy, just some simple suggestions from my own experience as a legislator in Sacramento and my district office in San Diego.

It seems to me if you are going to help the aging minorities, the first step is to put more effort into making sure that the aging in general get more attention from government. We cannot hope to influence aging policies, legislation, or programs with special considerations and preferences for the minority person if the aging policies, legislation, and programs don't even exist.

If there is no state policy on aging expressed by the executive and legislative branches of state government, it is impossible to assure ethnic considerations in that policy.

If there were no nutrition programs based on Older Americans Act Title VII, it would be impossible to get ethnic food preferences in proportion to the ethnic population at the nutrition sites.

If there were no legislation (AB 324) setting up state staffing for federal housing programs, it would be impossible to mandate bilingual personnel on that staff.

If there are no funds for multi-purpose senior centers, then it is impossible to set up a Mexican-American or Black or Asian senior center in the logical geographical areas.

The objective of our strategy must be two-fold: the minority (aging) and the minority within the minority (aging ethnic persons).

Many times in life a person gets a job or a promotion, is invited to an important and interesting event or gets some wonderful opportunity because of a personal friend's influence. This happens so often we commonly say "It's who you know that counts." We may not like this sort of thing! Of course, that depends on whether it is a plus or minus for us personally. But we all recognize that that is the way life is.

Since this is a reality, we have to use it to the advantage of older people. When it comes to legislation, the people who count are the legislators. Your access to a legislator is crucial in securing support for legislation. If all of you present were to develop a good relationship with your own legislators, you would be a tremendous force for aging. But, you must realize that a legislator is only one-half of the job. The other half is politician. Your asesmblyman, senators, congressmen, are legislator-politicians, or in election years, politician-legislators. You must work with them both— In season and out.

From the young and the old, the Harris Survey disclosed potential support for a movement to improve the conditions and social status of those over 65. Those under 65 are most conscious of the need for such a movement. Eighty-one percent of this group feel people need to join together to work toward improving conditions for people 65 and over, and 70 percent of the older group shared this feeling.

Substantial numbers would be interested in joining a group with these goals: the percentages from the survey who said they would "certainly" or "probably" join and take part represent 44.5 million of the 18-64 group, and 6.7 million of the 65 plus are potential for such an organization.

Thus, both young and old can identify with other older Americans as people sharing the same needs and problems of all humans.

You must mobilize yourselves with senior citizen organizations which have already been identified as a special interest group targeted for counting by politicians because one out of every three voters is 55 or over.

But, it is not enough just for the gerontologist to join with senior advocates. I suggest that you take, and encourage others to take, a visible and active role in legislative campaigns. It is one very effective way of gaining the indebtedness, the access to, the friendship of, and the loyalty of a legislator. If this involvement in legislative campaigns happens in assembly districts throughout the state, the seniors and people like yourselves who work with and for the seniors are bound to increase their influence.

If a candidate meets a volunteer in his campaign headquarters working for his re-election, stuffing envelopes, folding flyers, putting precinct kits together, phoning voters, walking precincts, he (the candidate) will not dismiss the interests and concerns of that individual. This is especially true if the volunteer has generated other volunteers and makes himself and his professional work known to the legislator. I am suggesting that involvement in the campaigns of legislators is a very basic and simple strategy.

Also, I suggest as another strategy the establishment of a "Watchdog Legislative Commitee" working with minority senior citizens, minority legislators and the Joint Committee on Aging to survey all aging legislation and evaluate it for provisions or absence of provisions related to the needs of minority older persons.

The assessment you make should be passed on to your professional friends, ethnic senior citizens groups, and your friends in the legislature.

Every aging bill should be looked at in the light of the special need of ethnic elderly and, where appropriate, amended to assure equitable attention for the minority elderly under the legislative proposal.

What I am really saying is: full citizen participation in the electoral and legislative process is the way to assure that government works for us. For the first time in the history of this country, the majority is turned off on politics and government—maybe for the first time the minority can be heard because we are just tuning in. We must encourage people to vote, to participate more than ever before!

There is no unique technique, no glamour or intrigue in strategies for "Affecting Legislative Priorities", for minorities. It is down to earth, common, basic, time-consuming, hard work— so obvious we often miss it.

1. **Support aging legislation** of benefit to all people.

2. **Develop an authentic rapport** with your politican-legislator "in season and out".

3. **Let the development happen on the streets** where you live and your legislator lives.

4. **Join forces with senior citizens** groups in your area.

5. **Establish a Watchdog Committee on Aging Legislation.**

Hopefully, these suggestions may be of some help. The only way you are going to get the things you want and need in Sacramento is to make your presence felt. You can't do it without getting involved in politics. If you ask me for a prediction about whether success is possible in assuring that the minority elderly get a priority in Sacramento, I am compelled to look to Mark Twain for an answer. He said, "I was gratified to be able to answer promptly, and I did. I said, I didn't know." But I do know that the prospects are not going to be any brighter unless those of you who say you are concerned about minority elderly and legislation pertaining to them put your energies and talents to work in a political way.

BIBLIOGRAPHY

BOOKS

Anderson, N. *The hobo: The sociology of the homeless.* Chicago: Phoenix Books, 1961.

Armstrong, Virginia Irving, & Turner, Frederick W., III (Eds.). *I have spoken: American history through the voices of the Indians.* Chicago: The Swallow Press, 1971.

Asian women. Berkeley: University of California, Berkeley, 1971.

Bakke, E. W. The unemployed worker. New Haven: Yale University Press, 1940 (b).

Baldwin, J. *The fire next time.* New York: Dial Press, 1963.

Balkemas, John B. *The aged in minority group: A bibliography.* Washington, D.C.: National Council on the Aged, 1973.

Barth, Gunther. *Bitter strength: History of Chinese in the United States.* Cambridge, Mass.: Harvard University Press, 1964.

Ben Broek, J. *Conference of the law of the poor.* San Francisco: Chandler, 1966.

Bessents, T. E. An aging Issei anticipates rejection. In G. Steward (Ed.), *Clinical studies in culture conflict.* New York: Ronald Press, 1958.

Bijou, S. W. Environment and intelligence: A behavioral analysis. In R. Cancro (Ed.), *Contributions to intelligence.* New York: Grune & Stratton, 1971.

Billingsley, Andrew. *Black families in White America.* Englewood Cliffs, N.J.: Prentice-Hall, 1968.

Blalock, H. *Toward a theory of minority group relations.* New York: Wiley & Sons, 1967.

Bogue, D. J. *Skid-row in American cities.* Chicago: Community and Family Study Center, University of Chicago, 1963.

Bosworth, Allan R. *America's concentration camps.* New York: Norton & Co., 1967.

Boulding, Kenneth E. *The impact of the social services.* New Brunswick, N.J.: Rutgers University Press, 1966.

Bourg, Carroll J. A social profile of Black aged in a southern, metropolitan area. *Proceedings of Research Conference on Minority Group Aged in the South, October, 1971.* Center for the Study of Aging and Human Development, Duke University Medical Center, Durham, North Carolina, April 1972, pp. 97-106.

Brenan, Jere L. *The forgotten American—American Indians remembered.* A selected bibliography for use in Social Work Education, New York. Council on Social Work Education, 1972.

Bulosan, Carlos. *American is in the heart.* New York: Harcourt, Brace & World, 1943. 65

Burgess, E. W., & Locke, J. J. *The family: From institution to companionship.* New York: American Book Co., 1945.

Cahn, Edgar S. *Our brother's keeper: The Indian in White America.* New York: World Book Publishing Co., 1969.

Carp, Frances M. *A future for the aged: Victoria Plaza and its residents.* Austin: University of Texas Press, 1966.

Carter, James H. Psychiatry, racism, and aging. *Proceedings of Research Conference on Minority Group Aged in the South, October 1971.* Center for the Study of Aging and Human Development, Duke University Medical Center, Durham, North Carolina, April 1972, pp. 125-30.

Cattell, R. B. *Abilities: Their structure, growth and action.* Boston: Houghton-Mifflin, 1972.

Cherry, C. *On human communication.* Cambridge, Mass.: Massachusetts Institute of Technology Press, 1966.

Clark, M. *Health in the Mexican-American culture.* Berkeley: University of California Press, 1959.

Clark, M., & Anderson, B. G. *Culture and aging: An anthropological study of older Americans.* Springfield, Ill.: Charles C. Thomas, 1967.

Cleaver, E. *Soul on ice.* New York: McGraw-Hill, 1968.

Cowgill, Donald O., & Holmes, L. O. (Eds.). *Aging and modernization.* New York: Appleton-Century-Crofts, 1972.

Daniels, Roger, & Kitano, Harry. *American racism.* Englewood Cliffs, N.J.: Prentice-Hall, 1970.

Davidson, C., & Gaitz, C. M. *Anglos, Blacks and Mexican-Americans in the southwest: Ethnic groups or castes?* Houston: Texas Research Institute of Mental Sciences, 1972. (Mimeographed.)

Davis, Allison, Gardner, Burleigh, B., & Gardner, Mary. *Deep South.* Chicago: University of Chicago, 1948.

Davis, D. Growing old Black. *Employment prospects of aged Blacks, Chicanos, and Indians.* Washington, D.C.: National Council on Aging, 1961.

Davis, Richard H. (Ed).. *Health services and the Mexican-American elderly.* Los Angeles: University of Southern California, Ethel Percy Andrus Gerontology Center, 1973.

Deutsch, C. P., & Deutsch, M. Brief reflections on the theory of early childhood enrichment programs. In R. O. Hes & R. H. Baer (Eds.), *Early education: Current theory, research, and action.* Chicago: Aldine, 1968.

66   DuBois, W. E. B. *The Philadelphia Negro.* New York: Benjamin Bloom, 1967. (Originally published, 1899.)

Duncan, O. D. A socioeconomic index for all occupations. In A. J. Reiss, Jr. (Ed.). *Occupations and social status.* New York: Free Press of Glencoe, 1961.

Elkins, Stanley M. *Slavery.* New York: Grosset & Dunlop, 1963.

Ellison, R. *The invisible man.* New York: Random House, 1952.

Federation of Experienced Americans and U.S. Human Resources Corporation. *The Spanish-speaking elderly poor. Part I: The assessment of demographic data and recommendations for the establishment of a national information center and three prototype centers.* Washington, D.C. & San Francisco, Calif.

Forbes, Jack D. *The Indian in America's past.* Englewood Cliffs, N.J.: Prentice-Hall, 1964.

Forbes, Jack D. *Native Americans of California and Nevada (a handbook).* Healdsburg, Calif.: Naturegraph Publishers, 1969.

Frazier, E. Franklin. *The Negro family in the U.S.* University Press, 1966.

Gans, H. *The urban villagers.* New York: Free Press of Macmillan, 1962.

Geist, H. *The psychological aspects of the aging process with sociological implications.* St. Louis: W. H. Green, 1968.

Gladwin, Little. *Poverty, U.S.A.* New York: Little, 1967.

Grier, W. H., & Cobbs, P. M. *Black rage.* New York: Basic Books, 1968.

Heer, David M. *Social statistics and the city.* Cambridge: Harvard University Press, 1968.

Hill, Robert. A profile of Black aged. *Proceedings of Research Conference on Minority Group Aged in the South, October 1971.* Center for the Study of Aging and Human Development, Duke University Medical Center, Durham, North Carolina, April 1972, pp. 92-96.

Hirsch, Carl. A review of findings on social and economic conditions of low-income Black and white aged for Philadelphia. *Proceedings of Research Conference on Minority Group Aged in the South, October 1971.* Center for the Study of Aging and Human Development, Duke University Medical Center, Durham, North Carolina, April 1972, pp. 63-8l.

Hosokawa, Bill. *Nisei: The quiet American.* New York: William Morrow, 1969.

Howe, L. K. *The white majority between poverty and affluence.* New York: Vintage Books, 1970.

Hsu, L. K. *The Oriental in America.* New York: Harper, 1967.

Hunter, R. *Poverty: Social conscience in the progressive era.* New York: Harper Torchbooks, 1965.

Israel, J. *Alienation from Marx to modern sociology.* Boston: Allyn & Bacon, 1971.

Jackson, Hobart C. The White House Conference on Aging and Black Aged. *Proceedings of Research Conference on Minority Group Aged in the South, October 1971* (J. J. Jackson, Ed.). Center for the Study of Aging and Human Development, Duke University Medical Center, Durham, North Carolina, April 1972, pp. 12-14.

Jackson, J. J. Family organization and ideology. In R. Dreger & K. Miller (Eds.), *Comparative studies of Negroes and whites in the United States, 1966-70.* New York: Academic Press, forthcoming, 1972.

Jackson, J. J. Research, training, service, and action concerns about Black aging and aged persons: An overview. *Proceedings of Research Conference on Minority Group Aged in the South, October 1971.* Center for the Study on Aging and Human Development, Duke University Medical Center, Durham, North Carolina, April 1972, pp. 41-47.

Jackson, J. J., & Davis, A., Jr. Characteristic patterns of aged rural Negroes in Macon County. In D. C. Johnson (Ed.), *A survey of selected socio-economic characteristics of Macon County, Alabama, 1965.* Tuskegee, Ala.: Macon County Community Action Office, 1966.

Jackson, Maurice. Social needs and research stances toward Black aged: An example from Los Angeles. *Proceedings of Research Conference on Minority Group Aged in the South, October 1971* (J. J. Jackson, Ed.). Center for the Study of Aging and Human Development, Duke University Medical Center, Durham, North Carolina, April 1972, pp. 82-83.

Jeffers, Camile. *Living poor.* Ann Arbor, Mich., 1967.

Kahl, J. *The measurement of modernism: A study of values in Brazil and Mexico.* Austin: University of Texas Press, 1968.

Kardner, Abraham, & Ovessey, Lionel. *Mark of oppression.* New York: W. W. Norton & Co., 1951.

Kastenbaum, Robert J. Psychological research concerns related to aging and aged Blacks. *Proceedings of Research Conference on Minority Group Aged in the South, October 1971* (J. J. Jackson, Ed.). Center for the Study of Aging and Human Development, Duke University Medical Center, Durham, North Carolina, April 1972, pp. 25-36.

Kastenbaum, Robert J. Uses of psychological and social data: A need for researchers as a springboard for action. *Proceedings of Research Conference on Minority Group Aged in the South, October 1971* (J. J. Jackson, Ed.). Center for the Study of the Aging and Human Development, Duke University Medical Center, Durham, North Carolina, April 1972, pp. 97-116.

Kent, Donald P., & Hirsch, Carl. Social and economic conditions of Negro and white aged residents of urban neighborhoods of low socio-economic status. *Needs and uses of services among Negro and white aged* (Vol. I). University Park: The Pennsylvania State University, 1971.

68   Kitano, Harry. *Japanese-Americans: The evolution of a subculture.* Englewood Cliffs, N.J.: Prentice-Hall, 1969.

Komarovsky, M. *The unemployed man and his family.* New York: Dryden Press, 1940.

Kreps, J. Economic status of the rural aged. In E. G. Youmans (Ed.), *Older rural Americans.* Lexington: University of Kentucky Press, 1967.

Kung, S. W. *Chinese in American life.* Seattle: University of Washington Press, 1962.

Lee, Rose Hom. *The Chinese in the United States of America.* Hong Kong: Hong Kong University Press, 1960.

Leichter, Hope J., & Mitchel, William E. *Kinship and casework.* New York: Russell Sage Foundation, 1967.

Levy, Jerrold E. The older American Indian. In E. Grant Youmans (Ed.), *Older rural Americans.* Lexington: University of Kentucky Press, 1967.

Lewis, H. *Blackways of Kent.* Chapel Hill: The University of North Carolina Press, 1955.

Lewis, Oscar. *The children of Sanchez.* New York: Random House, 1961.

Lopata, H. The function of voluntary associations in an ethnic community: Polonia. In E. Burgess & D. Bogue (Eds.), *Contributions to urban sociology.* Chicago: University of Chicago Press, 1965.

Lowenthal, M. F. *Aging and mental disorder in San Francisco.* San Francisco: Jossey-Bass, 1967.

Mackey, John E. (Ed.). *American Indian task force report.* New York: Council on Social Work Education, 1973.

Madsen, W. *The Mexican-Americans of South Texas.* New York: Holt, Rinehart & Winston, 1964.

Matson, F. W. The communication of welfare. In F. W. Matson & A. Montagu (Eds.), *The human dialogue.* New York: Free Press, 1967.

McDowell, Arthur. Health data on aging persons. *Proceedings of research conference on minority group aged in the South, October 1971* (J. J. Jackson, Ed.). Center for the Study of Aging and Human Development, Duke University Medical Center, Durham, North Carolina, April 1972, pp. 117-24.

McKenzie, Roderick D. *Oriental exclusion: The effect of American immigration laws, regulations and judicial decisions upon the Chinese and Japanese on the American Pacific Coast.* Chicago: University of Chicago Press, 1928.

Moore, B. M., & Holtzman, W. H. *Tomorrow's Parents.* Austin: University of Texas Press, 1965.

Morey, Sylvester M. *Can the red man help the white man?* New York: Gilbert Church Publications, 1970.

Moustafa, A. T., & Weiss, G. *Health status and practices of Mexican-Americans.* University of California, Mexican-American Study Project, Advance Report 11. Los Angeles: University of California, Los Angeles, 1968.

Munsell, Marvin R. Functions of the aged among Salt River Pima (Arizona). In Donald O. Cowgill & Lowell D. Holmes (Eds.), *Aging and modernization.* New York:: Appleton-Century-Crofts, 1972.

Nee, Victor G., & deBary, Brett. *Longtime Californian: A documentary study of an American Chinatown.* New York: Pantheon Books, 1973.

Niebanck, P. L. Knowledge gained in studies of relocation: A challenge to housing policy. *Proceedings of Research Conference on Patterns of Living and Housing of Middle-Aged and Older People.* Washington, D.C.: U.S. Government Printing Office, 1965.

Niebanck, P. L., & Pope, J. B. An overview of the national relocation population. In *The elderly in older urban areas.* Institute for Environmental Studies, University of Pennsylvania, 1965.

Norman, J. C. *Medicine in the ghetto.* New York: Appleton-Century-Crofts, 1969.

Nye, Ivan, & Rushing, William. Toward measurement research. In J. K. Hadden & M. L. Borgatta (Eds.), *Marriage and the family.* Itasca, Ill.: F. E. Peacock Publishers, 1969.

Pinkney, A. *Black Americans.* Englewood Cliffs, N.J.: Prentice-Hall, 1969.

Ploski, H. A., & Brown, R. E., Jr. *The Negro amlanac.* New York: Bellwether Publishing Co., 1967.

Pollard, Lulu. *Retirement: Black and white.* Jericho, N.Y.: Exposition Press, 1973.

Psychiatry and Public Affairs. GAP report. Chicago: Aldine Publishing Co., 1966.

Quinn, Galen W. Dentistry and aging persons. *Proceedings of Research Conference on Minority Group Aged in the South, October 1971* (J. J. Jackson, Ed.). Center for the Study of Aging and Human Development, Duke University Medical Center, Durham, North Carolina, April 1971, pp. 131-135.

Ramsey, Edward, Jr. Nutritional research, training, and services relative to aging aged Black. *Proceedings of Research Conference on Minority Group Aged in the South, October 1971* (J. J. Jackson, Ed.). Center for the Study of Aging and Human Development, Duke University Medical Center, Durham, North Carolina, April 1972, pp. 37-40a.

Randall, Ollie A. Protective services for older people. In *Seminar on protective services for older people.* New York: The National Council on Aging, 1964.

Reed, John, Howze, Glenn, & Ramsey, Edward, Jr. Prospects for developing gerontological training programs at Black institutions. *Proceedings of Research Conference on Minority Group Aged in the South, October 1971* (J. J. Jackson, Ed.). Center for the Study of Aging and Human Development, Duke University Medical Center, Durham, North Carolina, April 1972, pp. 145-47; 148-49; 150-51.

70   Reich, J. M., Stegman, M. A., & Stegman, N. W. *Relocating the dispossessed elderly: A study of Mexican-Americans.* Philadelphia: University of Pennsylvania Institute of Environmental Studies, 1966.

Report of the National Advisory Commission on Civil Disorders. New York: A Bantam Book, The New York Times Co., 1968.

Riessman, F., Cohen, J., & Pearl. A. *Mental health of the poor.* New York: The Crowell Collier Publishing Co., Free Press of Glencoe, 1964.

Riley, Matilda White, & Foner, Anne. *Aging and Society* (Vol. 1). New York: Russell Sage Foundation,

Rommey, A. K., & Kluckhohn, C. The Rimrock Navaho. In F. R. Kluckhohn & F. L. Strodtbeck (Eds.), *Variations in value orientations.* Evanston, Ill.: Row, Peterson & Co., 1961.

Rose, A. The sub-culture of aging. In A. Rose & W. A. Peterson (Eds.), *Old people and their social world.* Philadelphia: F. A. Davis, 1965.

Rosow, I. *Social integration of the aged.* New York: Free Press, 1967.

Ross, A. *The Hindu family in its urban setting.* Toronto: University of Toronto Press, 1961.

Rubenstein, Daniel I. Social participation of aged Blacks: A national sample. *Proceedings of Research Conference on Minority Group Aged in the South, October 1971* (J. J. Jackson, Ed.). Center for the Study of Aging and Human Development, Duke University Medical Center, Durham, North Carolina, April 1972, pp. 48-62.

Sarasvati, P. R. *The high-caste Hindu woman.* Philadelphia: James B. Rodgers Printing Co., 1888.

Saunders, L. *Cultural differences and medical care: The case of the Spanish-speaking people of the southwest.* New York: Russell Sage Foundation, 1954.

Scanzoni, John H. *The Black family in modern society.* Boston: Allyn & Bacon, 1971.

Schapera, I. *Married life in an African tribe.* New York: Scheridan House, 1941.

Schwartz, W. Neighborhood centers and group work. In H. S. Maas (Ed.), *Research in the social sciences: A five-year review.* New York: National Association of Social Workers, 1971.

Seligman, B. B. *Aspects of poverty.* New York: Thomas Y. Crowell Co., 1968.

Shanas, E., Townsend, P., Wedderburn, D., Frils, H., Mihoj, P., & Stehouwer, J. *Old people in three industrial societies.* New York: Atherton Press, 1968.

Sheldon, H. D. *The older population of the United States.* New York: John Wiley & Sons, 1958.

Sheppard, H. L. Age and migration factors in the socio-economic conditions of urban Black and white women. In *New perspective on older workers.* Kalamazoo, Mich.: The W. E. Upjohn Institute, 1971.

Simmel, George. The metropolis in mortal life. In Kurt H. Wolff (Ed.), *The Sociology of George Simmel.* Glencoe, Ill.: The Free Press, 1950.

Simmons, Leo. Aging in preindustrial societies. In Clark Tibbitts (Ed.), *Handbook of gerontology.* Chicago: University of Chicago Press, 1960.

Smith, Stanley H. The older rural Negro. In E. Grant Youmans (Ed.), *Older rural Americans.* Lexington: University of Kentucky Press, 1967.

Solomon, B. J. Ethnicity, mental health, and the older Black aged. In *Ethnicity, mental health and aging.* Los Angeles: The Gerontology Center, University of Southern California, 1970.

Spradley, J. P. *You owe yourself a drunk: The ethnography of urban nomads.* Boston: Little, Brown & Co., 1970.

Stanford, E. P. *Minority Aging.* Institute on Minority Aging Proceedings. San Diego: Center on Aging, School of Social Work, San Diego State University, 1974,

Stanford, E. P. *Minority Aging.* Second institute on Minority Aging Proceedings. San Diego: Center on Aging, School of Social Work, San Diego State University, 1975.

Steinfield, Melvin. *Cracks in the melting pot—racism and discrimination in American history.* Beverly Hills: Glencoe Press, 1970.

Strauss, A. *The American city: A sourcebook of urban imagery.* Chicago: Aldine Publishing Co., 1968.

Szafran, J. Psycho-physiological studies of aging in pilots. In G. A. Talland (Ed.), *Human aging and behavior.* New York: Academic Press, 1968.

Tachicki, Amy, Wong, Eddie, Odo, Franklin, & Wong, Buck (Eds.). *Roots: An Asian-American reader.* Los Angeles: University of California, Los Angeles, 1971.

Thomas, P. *Indian women through the ages.* New York: Asia Publishing House, 1964.

Thomas, W. I., & Znaniecki, F. *The polish peasant in Europe and America.* New York: Dover Publications, 1958.

Thornton, R. J., & Nam, C. B. The lower mortality rates of non-whites at the older ages: An enigma in demographic analysis. In *Research reports in social science* (Vol. 2). Tallahassee: Florida State University, Institute for Social Research, 1968.

Thune, Jeanne M. *Group protraits in Black and white.* Nashville, Senior Citizens, Inc., 1969.

72 Townsend, P. *The family life of old people: An inquiry in East London.* HammondsWorth: Pelican Books—A634, 1963.

Townsend, P., & Wedderburn, D. *The aged in the welfare state.* London: G. Bell & Sons, 1965.

von Mering, O., & Weniger, F. Social-cultural background of the aging individual. In J. E. Birren (Ed.), *Handbook of aging and the individual.* Chicago: University of Chicago Press, 1959.

Weeks, A. *The urban aged: Race and medical care.* Ann Arbor, Mich.: University of Michigan School of Public Health, Research Series No. 14, 1968.

Youmans, E. G. *Older rural Americans.* Kentucky: University of Kentucky Press, 1967.

ARTICLES AND JOURNALS

Ablon, Joan. Relocated Indians in the San Francisco Bay area. *Human Organization,* 1964, *23,* 296-304.

Arth, Malcolm. Aging: A cross-cultural perspective. In *Research Planning and action for the elderly: The power and potentials of social sciences.* New York: Behavior Publications, Inc.

Asayama, S. Comparison of sexual development of American and Japanese Adolescents. *Psychologia,* 1957, 129-131.

Bader, Jeanne E. A conglomerate of information—with social and cultural overtones. 1973 (mimeographed).

Baratz, J. C., & Baratz, S. S. Early childhood intervention: The social science base of institutional racism. *Harvard Educational Review,* 1970, *40,* 29-50.

Barg, Sylvia K., & Hirsch, Carl. A successor model for community support of low-income minority group aged. *Aging and human development,* 1972, *3,* 243-252.

Barg, Sylvia K., & Hirsch, Carl. Neighborhood service support networks: A alternative for the maintenance of active community residence by low-income minority group aged in the inner city. Paper presented at the 27th Annual Meeting of the Gerontological Society, Portland, Oregon, October 29-November 1, 1974.

Barron, Milton L. Minority group characteristics of the aged in American society. *Journal of Gerontology,* 1953, *8,* 477-482.

Beattie, Walter M., Jr. The aging Negro: Some implications for social welfare services. *Phylon,* 1960, *21,* 131.

Bennett, C. G., Tokuyama, G. H., and Bruyer, R. P. Health of Japanese-Americans in Hawaii. *Public Health Reports,* United States Public Health Service, pp. 753-762.

Berado, F. Social adaptation to widowhood among a rural-urban aged population. *Washington State College Agricultural Experiment Station Bulletin,* No. 689, 1967.

Birren, James E. The abuse of the urban aged. *Psychology Today,* 1970, *3*(10), 36-38.

Bogardus, E. S. Filipino immigrant attitudes. *Sociology and Social Research,* May-June, 1930, *14,* 469-479.

Breslow, Lester, & Klein, Bonnie. Health and race in California. *Journal of Public Health,* 1971, *61,* 763-775.

Brill, N. Q., Weinstein, R., & Garratt, J. Poverty and mental illness: Patients' perception of poverty as an etiological factor in their illness. *American Journal of Psychiatry,* 1966, *125,* 1172-1179.

Brody, E. B. Cultural exclusion, character and illness. *American Journal of Psychiatry,* 1966, *122,* 852-858.

Brody, Elaine M. (MSSA), & Brody, Stanley J. (MSSA,JD). A ninety-minute inquiry: The expressed needs of the elderly. *The Gerontologist,* Summer 1970, *10*(2): 99-106.

Broom, L., & Shevky, E. Mexicans in the United States: A problem in social differentiation. *Sociology and Social Research,* 1952, *36,* 150-158.

Brunswick, Ann F. What generation gap? A comparison of some generational differences among Blacks and whites. *Social Problems,* 1969-1970, *17,* 358-370.

Carp, Frances M. (Ph.D.). Communicating with elderly Mexican-Americans. *The Gerontologist,* Summer 1970, *10*(2), 126-133.

Carp, Frances M. Housing and minority group elderly. *The Gerontologist,* 1969, *9,* 20-24.

Carp, Frances M. Some determinants of low application rate of Mexican-American for Public housing for the elderly. In press.

Carter, J. H. Psychiatry, racism, and aging. *Journal of the American Geriatric Society,* *20,* 343-346.

Catapusan, B. T. Leisure time problems of Filipino immigrants. *Sociology and Social Research,* July 1940, *24,* 541-549.

Caudill, W., & Scarr, H. A. Japanese value orientation and culture change. *Ethnology,* 1962, *1,* 53-91.

Chandler, Albert R. The traditional Chinese attitude toward old age. *Journal of Gerontology,* 1949-1950, *4-5.*

Chen, Pei-Ngo. The Chinese community in Los Angeles. *Social Casework,* December 1970, *51,* 591-598.

Chen, Pei-Ngo. Sampans in California. *Social Work,* March 1973, *18,* 41-48.

Chen, S. C., & J. L. Chen. Effects of culture on the success of aging: A preliminary study comparing the productivity of two aging groups of Chinese and American men. *Boston Medical Quarterly,* 1964, *15,* 4-22.

74   Clark, Margaret. Patterns of aging among the elderly poor of the inner city. *The Gerontologist,* Spring 1971, *11,* (1,2), 58-66.

Clark, Margaret, & Mendelson, Monique. Mexican-American aged in San Francisco: A Case description. *The Gerontologist,* Summer 1969, *9*(2), 90-95.

Clemente, Frank, Rexroad, P. A., & Hirsch, C. Participation of Black aged in voluntary associations. *Journal of Gerontology,* 1975, *30*(4), 469-472.

Clemente, Frank, & Sauer, W. J. Race and morale of urban aged. *The Gerontologist,* 1974, *14*(4), 342-344.

Coiro, C. Why the national caucus on the Black aged. *Harvest Years,* 1971, *11,* 13-18.

Comfort, A. Biological theories of aging. *Human Development,* 1970, *13,* 127-139.

Crouch, Ben M. Age and institutional support: Perceptions of older Mexican-Americans. *Journal of Gerontology,* 1972, *27,* 524-529.

Deshane, M. R. Grounded theory in gerontology—crucial need for training professionals in the future. *The Gerontologist,* 1972, *12*(3), 72.

Dohrenwend, B. P. Social status and psychological disorders: An issue of substance and an issue of method. *American Sociological Review,* 1966, *31,* 14-34.

Domeny, P., & Grinrich, P. A reconsideration of Negro-white mortality differentials in the United States. *Demography,* 1967, *4,* 820-837.

Dominick, Joan. Mental patients in nursing homes: Four ethnic influences. *Journal of American Geriatric Society,* 1969, *17,* 634.

Eisdorfer, C. Patterns of federal funding for research in aging. *The Gerontologist,* 1968, *8,* 3-6.

Enrlich, Ira F. Toward a social profile of aged Black population in the United States—Exploratory study. *Aging and Human Development,* 1973, *4*(3), 271-276.

Epstein, L. J. The network and urban social organization. *Rhodes-Livingstone Institute Journal,* 1961, *29,* 29-62.

Erikson, E. H. The concept of identity in race relations: Notes and queries. *Daedalus,* 1966, *95* (The Negro American, Part II), 145-171.

Flynn, John P. (ACSW). The team approach: A possible control for the single service schism: An exploratory study. *The Gerontologist,* Summer 1970, *10*(2), 119-124.

Fong, Stanley, Assimilation of Chinese in America: Changes in orientation and social perception. *American Journal of Sociology,* 1970, *63,* 265-273.

Friedman, P., & Phillips, G. M. Toward a rhetoric for the poverty class. *Journal of Communication,* 1967, *17,* 234-249.

Gaitz, C. M., & Scott, J. Mental health of Mexican-Americans—do ethnic factors make a difference? *Geriatrics,* 1974, *29*(11), 103.

Geagin, J. R. The kinship ties of Negro urbanites. *Social Science Quarterly,* 1968, *69,* 660-665.

Geagin, J. R. A note on the friendship ties of Black urbanites. *Social Forces,* 1970, *49,* 303-308.

The Gerontologist, Summer 1970, *10*(2) (entire issue).

The Gerontologist, Spring 1971, *11*(1) (entire issue).

The Gerontologist, 1973 (entire issue).

Gerson, W. M. Mass media socialization behavior: Negro-white differences. *Social Forces,* 1966, *45,* 40-50.

Goldstein, Sidney. Home tenure and expenditure patterns of the aged, 1960-61. *The Gerontologist,* 1968, *8,* 17-24.

Goldstein, Sidney. Negro-white differentials in consumer problems of the aged, 1960-61. *The Gerontologist,* 1971, *11,* 242-249.

Hacker, H. M. Women as a minority group. *Social Forces,* 1951, *30,* 60-69.

Hearn, H. L. Career and leisure patterns of middle-aged urban Blacks. *The Gerontologist,* 1971, *11*(4), 21-26.

Hechter, H. M., & Borhani, N. O. Longevity in racial groups differs. *California Health,* February 1965, *20*(15),

Heiskanan, Veronica Stolte. The myth of the middle-class in American family sociology. *The American Sociologist,* February 1971, *6*(1), 14-18.

Henderson, G. The Negro recipient of OAA, results of discrimination. *Social Casework,* 1965, *46,* 208-214.

Heyman & Jeffers. Study of the relative influence of race and socio-economic status upon the activities and attitudes of a southern aged population. *Journal of Gerontology,* 1964, *19,* 225-229.

Hill, Charles A., Jr. Measures of longevity of American Indians. *Public Health Reports,* 1970, *85,* 233-239.

Himes, Joseph, & Hamlett, Margaret. The assessment of adjustment of aged Negro women in a southern city. *Phylon,* Summer 1962, *23,* 139-148.

Hirsch, C., Kent, D. P., & Silverman, S. L. Homogeneity and heterogeneity among low-income Negro and white aged. *Research Planning Action for the Elderly: The Power and Potentials of Social Sciences.* Behavioral Publications Inc., New York, pp. 484-500.

76   Hsu, Francis L. K. *Clan, Caste and Club.* Chicago: Van Nostrand.

Hunt, C. Private integrated housing in a medium-size American city. *Social Problems,* 1960, *7,* 196-209.

Isenberg, B. To be old and poor is to be alone, afraid, ill-fed and unknown. *Wall Street Journal,* November 15, 1972 (a).

Jackson, H. C. National goals and priorities in the social welfare of aging. *The Gerontologist,* 1971, *2,* 226-231.

Jackson, Jacqueline J. Aged Blacks: A potpourri towards the reduction of racial inequities. *Phylon,* 1971, *32,* 260-280.

Jackson, Jacqueline J. Aged Negroes: Their cultural departures from statistical stereotypes and rural-urban differences. *The Gerontologist,* Summer 1970, *10*(2), 140-145.

Jackson, Jacqueline J. The Blacklands of gerontology. *Aging and human Development,* 1967, *2,* 168-178.

Jackson, Jacqueline J. Comparative lifestyles and family relationships among older Black women. *The Family Coordinator,* forthcoming.

Jackson, Jacqueline J. Help me, somebody! I'm an old Black standing in the need of institutionalizing! *Psychiatric Opinion,* 1973, *10*(6), 6-16.

Jackson, Jacqueline J. Kinship relations among Negro Americans. *Journal of Social and Behavioral Sciences,* 1970, *16,* 5-17.

Jackson, Jacqueline J. Marital patterns among aging Blacks. *The Family Coordinator,* 1972, *21,* 27.

Jackson, Jacqueline J. National caucus on the Black aged: A progress report. *Aging and Human Development,* 1971-c, *2,* 226-231.

Jackson, Jacqueline J. National council on the Black Aged, Black Aged and Politics. *The Annals,* September 1974, *415,* 146-147.

Jackson, Jacqueline J. Negro aged and social gerontology: A critical gerontology. *Journal of Social and Behavioral Sciences,* 1968, *13,* 42-47.

Jackson, Jacqueline J. Negro aged: Toward needed research in social gerontology. *The Gerontologist,* Spring 1971, *11*(1-2), 52-57.

Jackson, Jacqueline J. Sex and social class variations in Negro older parent-adult child relationships. *Aging and Human Development,* 1971, *2,* 96-107.

Jackson, Jacqueline J. Social gerontology and the Negro: A review. *The Gerontologist,* 1967, *7,* 168-178.

Jackson, Jacqueline J., & Ball, M. A comparison of rural and urban Georgia aged Negroes. *Journal of the Association of Social Science Teachers,* 1966, *12,* 30-37.

Jacobs, J. Ethnographic study of a retirement setting. *The Gerontologist,* 1974, *14*(6), 483-487.

Jenkins, M. M. Age and migration factors in the socioeconomic conditions of urban Blacks and urban White women. *Industrial Gerontology,* 1971, *9,* 13-17.

Kalish, Richard A. A gerontological look at ethnicity, human capacities, and individual adjustment. *The Gerontologist,* Spring 1971, *11*(1-2), 78-87.

Kalish, Richard A., & Moriwaki, Sharon. The world of the elderly Asian American. *Journal of Social Issues,* 1973, *29*(2), 187-209.

Kalish, Richard A., & Yuen, Sam. Americans of East Asian ancestry: Aging and the aged. *The Gerontologist,* Spring 1971, *11*(1-2), 36-47.

Karno, Marvin, & Edgerton, R. Perceptions of mental illness in a Mexican-American community. *Archives of General Psychiatry,* 1969, *20,* 233-238.

Karno, Marvin, Ross, R. N., & Caper, R. A. Mental health role of physicians in a Mexican-American community. *Community Mental Health Journal,* 1969, *5,* 62-69.

Kastenbaum, R. A special issue—Black aging. *Aging and Human Development,* 1971, *2,* 155 231.

Kent, Donald P. The elderly in minority groups: Variant patterns of aging. *The Gerontologist,* Spring 1971, *11*(1-2), 26-29.

Kent, Donald P. The Negro aged. *The Gerontologist,* Spring 1971, *11*(1-2), 48-5l.

Kent, D. P., Hirsch, C., & Barg, Sylvia K. Indigenous workers as a crucial link in the total support system for low-income, minority group aged. *Aging and Human Development,* 1971, *2,* 189-196 (*2,* 208-209).

Kiefer, C. W. Notes on anthropology and the minority elderly. *The Gerontologist,* 1971, *11*(1-2), 94-98.

Killian, L., & Hoer, J. Variables related to attitudes regarding school desegregation among white southerners. *Sociometry,* 1958, *21,* 159-164.

Kim, Bok-Lim C. Asian Ameriancs: No model minority. *Social Work,* May 1973, *18,* 44-53.

Koenig, R., Goldner, N. S., Kresojovich, R., & Lockwood, G. Ideas about illness of elderly Black and white in an urban hospital. *Aging and Human Development,* 1971, *2,* 217-225.

Lacklen, C. Aged, Black and poor: Three case studies. *Aging and Human Development,* 1971, *2,* 202-207.

LaCrosse, E. R., Lee, P. C., Litman, F., Olgivie, D. M., Stodolsky, S. S., & White, B. L. The first six years of life: A report on current research and educational practice. *Genetic Psychology Monographs,* 1970, *82,* 161-266.

78
Lambing, Mary L. B. Social class living patterns of retired Negroes. *The Gerontologist,* *12*(3). 285-288.

Lawton, M. Powell, & Cohen, J. Environment and well-being of elderly inner-city residents. *Environment and Behavior,* 1974, *6*(2), 194-211.

Leonard, O. E. The older rural Spanish-speaking people of the Southwest. *Older Rural Americans,* by E. G. Youmans, University of Kentucky Press, 1967.

Lifter, M. L., & Morrisey, P. Personality differences between typical urban Negroes and whites. *Journal of Negro Education,* 1971, *40,* 66-75.

Lipman, Aaron, & Lipman & Hraden. Miami concerted baseline study. *The Gerontologist,* December 1965, *5*(4), 256.

Lipman, Aaron, & Lipman & Harden. Preparation for death in old age. *Journal of Gerontology,* 1966, *21,* 426-431.

Lipman, Aaron, & Lipman & Harden. Responsibility and moral. *Proceedings of 7th International Congress of Gerontology,* Vienna, 1966, pp. 267-276.

Lopata, H. Z. Widows as a minority group. *The Gerontologist,* Spring 1971, *11*(1-2), 67-77.

Lowenthal, M. Antecedents of isolation and mental illness in old age. *Archives of General Psychiatry,* 1965, *12,* 245-254.

McCaslin, Rosemary (MA), & Calvert, Welton R. (MA). Social indicators in Black and white: Some ethnic considerations in delivery of service to the elderly. *Journal of Gerontology,* 1975, *30*(1), 60-66.

McKevin, Tony P., & Rosencranz, Howard A. Racial differences in life satisfaction and adjustment between welfare and non-welfare non-institutionalized, aged males. *Proceedings of the 20th Annual Meeting of the Gerontological Society,* 1967.

Maddox, George E. Factor arti-fact. *Human Development,* 1965, *8,* 117.

Maldonado, David, Jr. The Chicano aged. *Social Work,* May 1975, *20*(3), 213-216.

Masuda, Minory, Matsumoto, Gary H., & Meredith, Gerald M. Ethnic identity in three generations of Japanese Americans. *The Journal of Social Psychology,* 1970, *81,* 199-207.

Mead, Margaret. Ethnological aspects of aging. *Psychosomatics,* 1967, *8*(4), 33-37.

Metropolitan Life Insurance Company. Trends in mortality of non-whites. *Statistical Bulletin,* 1970, *51,* 5-8.

Metropolitan Life Insurance Company. Mortality differentials among non-white groups. *Statistical Bulletin,* July 1974.

Modell, John. The Japanese American family: A perspective for future investigations. *Pacific Historical Review,* 1968, *36,* 67-81.

Moore, Joan W. Mexican-Americans. *The Gerontologist,* Spring 1971, *11*(1-2), 30-35.

Moore, Joan W. Situational factors affecting minority aging. *The Gerontologist,* 1971, *11* (1-2), 88-93.

Morales, Armando. Mental and public health issues: The case of Mexican Americans in Los Angeles. *El Grito,* 1970, *3,* 3-11.

Morgan, Robert F. The adult growth examination: Preliminary comparisons of physical aging in adults by sex and race. *Preceptial and motor Skills,* 1968, *27,* 595-599.

National Center on the Black Aged, Inc. Deplorable condition of housing for aged Blacks. *NCBA Technical Bulletin Series,* August 1975, n.p.

National Center on the Black Aged, Inc. Thirty-seven percent of Black aged in poverty in 1973. *NCBA Technical Bulletin Series,* June 1975, n.p.

Okada, Y. Changing family relationships of older people. Japan during the last fifty years. In C. Tibbitts and W. Donahue (Eds.), *Social and psychological aspects of aging.* New York: Columbia University Press, 1962.

Older Japanese changing ways. *New York Times,* November 7, 1974.

Olsen, M. E. Social and political participation of Blacks. *American Sociological Review,* 1970, *35,* 682-697.

Orshanksy, Mollie. The aged Negro and his income. *Social Security Bulletin,* February 1964, *27,*

Orshanksy, Mollie. The poor in the city and suburb. *Social Security Bulletin,* 1966, *29,* 3-29.

Pacific Citizen. Official Publication of the Japanese American Citizens League. Published weekly. 125 Weller Street, Los Angeles, CA 90012.

Palmore, Erdman. The status and integration of the aged in Japanese society. *Journal of Gerontology,* 1975, *30,* 199-208.

Palmore, Erdman. Variables related to needs among the aged poor. *Journal of Gerontology,* 1971, *26,* 524-531.

Palmore, Erdman, & Whittington, F. Differential trends toward equality between whites and non-whites. *Social Forces,* 1970, *49,* 108-117.

Price, John A. The migration and adaptation of American Indians to Los Angeles. *Human Organization,* 1968, *27,* 168-175.

Reynolds, David K., & Kalish, Richard A. Anticipation of futurity as a function of ethnicity and age. (Blacks, whites, Japanese-Americans, and Chicanos.) *Journal of Gerontology,* 1974, *29,* 224-231.

80   Rice, Carolyn. Old and Black. *Harvest Years,* November 1968, *8,* 24-47.

Richek, M. G., Chuculate, O., & Klinert, D. Aging and ethnicity in healthy elderly women. *Geriatrics,* 1971, *26,* 146-152.

Rojo, F. A. Social Maladjustment among filipinos in the United States. *Sociology and Social Research,* May 1937, *21,* 447-457.

Ramano, Octavio. The anthropology and sociology of the Mexican-American: The Distortion of Mexican-American history. *El Grito,* Fall 1968.

Rosow, Irving. Retirement housing and social integration. *The Gerontologist,* June 1961, *1*(2).

Rubel, Arthur J. Concepts of disease in Mexican-American culture. *American Anthropologist,* 1960, *62,* 795-814.

Rubenstein, D. I. An examination of social participation found among a national sample of Black and white elderly. *Aging and Human Development* 1971, *2,* 172-188.

Schein, E. The Chinese indoctrination program for prisoners of war. *Psychiatry,* 1956, *19,* 149-172.

Schonfield, D. What's so different about being old? *On Growing Old/Vivre Longtemps,* 1969, *7,* 1-5.

Schultz, C. B., & Aurbach, H. A. The usefulness of cumulative deprivation as an explanation of educational deficiencies. *Merrill-Palmer Quarterly,* 1971, *17,* 27-39.

Seeman, M. On the meaning of alienation. *American Sociological Review,* 1959, *24,* 783-791.

Shanas, E. Measuring the home health needs of the aged in five countries. *Journal of Gerontology,* 1971, *26,* 37-40.

Simos, Bertha G. (DSW). Relations of adults with aging parents. Paper presented at the 8th International Congress of Gerontology, Washington, August 1969. *The Gerontologist,* Summer 1970, *10*(2), *135-139.*

Slater, P. E. Cultural attitudes toward the aged. *Journal of Human Relations,* 1967, *15,* 169-179.

Smith, T. Lynn. The changing number and distribution of the aged Negro population of the U.S. *Phylon,* 1967, *18,* 339.

Snow, C. P. The two cultures controversy. *Encounter,* 1960, *15,* 64-68.

Sparks, P. M. Behavioral versus experiential aging: Implications for intervention. *The Gerontologist,* 1973, *13,* 15-18.

Staples, R. Towards a sociology of the Black family: A theoretical and methodological assessment. *Journal of Marriage and Family Living,* 1971, *33,* 119-138.

Streib, Gordon F. Are the aged a minority group? In A. W. Goulder and S. W. Miller (Eds.), *Applied sociology*. Glencoe, Ill.: The Free Press, 1965.

Stringfellow, W. The representation of the poor in American society. *Law and Contemporary Problems,* 1966, *31,* 142-151.

Swanson, W. C., & Harter, C. L. How do elderly Blacks cope in New Orleans? *Aging and Human Development,* 1971, *2,* 210-216.

Talley, T., & Kaplan, J. The Negro aged. *Newsletter,* Gerontological Society, December 3, 1956.

Taylor, B. J., & Peach, W. N. Social and economic characteristics of elderly Indians in Phoenix, Arizona. *Journal of Economics and Business,* 1974, *26*(2), 151-155.

Thune, Jeanne M. Racial attitudes of older adults. *The Gerontologist,* Stptember 1967, *7* (3), Part I, 179.

Tissue, T. Social class and the senior citizen center. *The Gerontologist,* 1971, *11,* 196-200.

Waddell, Jack O., & Watson, O. M. (Eds.). *The American Indian in urban society.* Boston: Little, Brown, 1971.

Watson, J. S. Cognitive-perceptual development in infancy: Setting for the seventies. *Merrill-Palmer Quarterly,* 1971, *17,* 139-152.

Webber, I. L., Coombs, D. W., & Hollings, J. S. Variations in value orientations by age in developing society. *Journal of Gerontology,* 1974, *29*(6), 676-683.

Weihl, Hannah. Jewish aged of different cultural origin in israel. A revision of a paper presented at the International Congress of Gerontology held in Washington in August, 1969. *The Gerontologist,* Summer 1970, *10*(2), 146-150.

White, Anthony C. An urban minority: Japanese Americans. Council of Planning Libraries Exchange Bibliography. No. 478, Monticello.

Wylie, F. M. Attitudes toward aging and the aged among Black Americans: Some historical perspectives. *Aging and Human Development,* 1971, *2,* 66-70.

Youmans, E. G. Family disengagement among older urban and rural women. *Journal of Gerontology,* 1967, *22,* 209-211.

Youmans, E. G. Objective and subjective economic disengagement among older rural and urban men. *Journal of Gerontology,* 1966, *21,* 439-411.

AMERICAN INDIAN NEWSPAPERS

Akwesasne Notes. Roosevelt, New York 13683.

The Navajo Times. Box 428, Window Rock, Arizona 86515.

Wassaja. 1451 Masonic Avenue, San Francisco, California 94117.

The aging and aged Blacks. Reports of the Special Concerns Sessions, 1971 White House Conference on Aging. Washington, D.C.: U.S. Government Printing Office.

The Asian-American elderly. Reports of the Special Concerns Sessions, 1971 White House Conference on Aging. Washington, D.C.: U.S. Government Printing Office.

Californians of Japanese, Chinese and Filipino ancestry: Population, employment income, education. San Francisco: State of California, Department of Industrial Relations, Division of Fair Employment Practices, June 1965.

Cohen, Felix. *Federal Indian law.* Washington, D.C.: U.S. Government Printing Office, 1958.

Conference and workshop on the Indian senior. (A report), February 19-23, 1973, Department of Sociology, San Diego State University.

David, D. Growing old Black. *Employment prospects of aged Blacks, Chicanos, and Indians.* Washington, D.C.: National Council on Aging, 1961.

Department of Health, Education and Welfare. *Alcoholism: A high priority health problem.* Task Force on Alcoholism. Washington, D.C.: U.S. Government Printing Office, 1968-1970.

Department of Health, Education and Welfare. *Facts about older Americans.* AoA Publication No. 310, May 1966.

Department of Housing and Urban Development. See various publications such as: *Population, Housing and Income and Federal Housing Programs.* Washington, D.C.: U.S. Government Printing Office, 1971.

Department of Interior. *Code of federal regulations—Title 25, Indians.* Washington, D.C.: U.S. Government Printing Office, 1965.

The elderly Indian. Reports of the Special Concerns Sessions, 1971 White House Conference on Aging. Washington, D.C.: U.S. Government Printing Office.

The elderly Indian. *Toward a national policy on aging.* 1971 White House Conference on Aging, Final Report Volume II. Washington, D.C.: U.S. Government Printing Office, 1973.

Epstein, Lenore A., & Murray, Janet H. The aged population of the U.S. *The 1963 Social Security Survey of the Aged* U.S. Department of Health, Education and Welfare, Social Administration, Office of Research and Statistics, Research Report No. 19.

Ethnic participation in operation mainstream: Program totals for the state of California. U.S. Department of Labor, Manpower Administration..

Fact sheet: Cuban Refugee Program. Prepared by U.S. Department of Health, Education and Welfare, S.R.S., Cuban Refugee Program, April 1972.

Geographic distribution of resettlement of Cuban refugees: January 1961-January 1971. Cuban Refugee Program.

Hearings before the Special Committee on Aging, U.S. Senate. *Advisory Council on the Elderly American Indian.* Washington, D.C.: U.S. Government Printing Office, 1971.

Hearings before the Special Committee on Aging, U.S. Senate. *Availability and usefulness of federal programs and services to elderly Mexican-Americans, 1-4.* 1968-1969.

Hearings before the Special Committee on Aging, U.S. Senate. *Training needs in Gerontology.* 93rd Congress, First Session, Part I, June 19, 1973. Washington, D.C.: U.S. Government Printing Office, 1973.

Hearings before the Special Committee on Aging, U.S. Senate. *Usefulness of the model cities program to the elderly.* 90th Congress, Second Session, Part II and III. Seattle, Washington, October 14, 1968 and Ogden, Utah, October 14, 1968.

Housing Statistics: Tables regarding total annual income of subsidized families who moved into Section 236 Housing by Status as Elderly Minority Groups, October 1, 1971-March 31, 1972 and total annual income of subsidized families who moved into Section 236 Housing by Status as Elderly and Number of Workers and Minority Group Cagetory. U.S. Government Report.

Kerri, James N. *American Indians (U.S. and Canada): A bibliography of contemporary studies and urban research.* Council of Planning Librarians Exchange Bibliography, Nos. 376 and 377. Monticello, Illinois, 1971.

Kerri, James N. *American Indians (U.S. and Canada): A bibliography of contemporary studies and urban research: Supplement to council of Planning Librarians Exchange Bibliographies Nos. 376-377.* Council of Planning Librarians Exchange Bibliographies, No. 594. Monticello, Illinois, 1971.

Lindsey, Inabel, B. *The Multiple hazards of aged and race: The situation of aged Blacks in the United States.* Report No. 92-450. Washington, D.C.: U.S. Government Printing Office, 1971.

Lopata, H. Z. Social and family relations of Black and white widows in urban communities. Washington, D.C.: Administration on Aging Publications No. 25, U.S. Department of Health, Education and Welfare.

Nosotros, Los Mexican Americanos. Bureau of the Census, U.S. Department of Commerce, 1970.

Nutrition for inner city aged: An interim report. Nutrition Series 14-A, Washington, D.C.: Administration on Aging.

The older person at home—a potential isolate or participant. National Institute of Mental Health, *Research utilization in aging, an exploration.* Proceedings of a conference sponsored by Community Research and Services Branch, April 30, 1963. Washington, D.C.: U.S. Government Printing Office, 1964.

84   Palmetier, Howard. Assistance to refugees in the United States. Department of HEW, SRS, presented before the U.S. Senate Appropriations Subcommittee on Foreign Operations, March 2, 1972.

President's Commission on Income Maintenance Program. *Poverty amid plenty: The American paradox.* Washington, D.C.: U.S. Government Printing Office, 1969.

Reynoso, Cruz, & Coopelman, Peter. Availability and usefulness of federal programs and services to elderly Mexican Americans: Proposal to eliminate the legal barriers. U.S. Senate Hearing, May 1972.

Significant titles on the American Indian (reprints of books and journals). New York: Johnson Reprint Corporation, 1973.

The Spanish-speaking elderly. Reports of the Special Concerns Sessions, 1971. 1971 White House Conference on Aging. Washington, D.C.: U.S. Government Printing Office.

State social welfare board, position statement: Issues: Aliens in California. A report by the state of California Health and Welfare Agency, Department of Social Welfare, January 1973.

Toward a national policy on aging. Final Report I and II, 1971 White House Conference on Aging, Department of HEW, SRS, 1973.

U.S. Congress. Senate. Special Committee on Aging. *Pre-White House Conference on Aging, summary of development and data: A report, together with minority and supplemental views.* Washington, D.C.: U.S. Government Printing Office, 1971.

U.S. Senate. 92nd Congress, First Session, 1971. *Special Committee on Aging. A statement by the members of the Advisory Council on the Elderly American Indian, together with an analysis of available statistical information and other appendixes.* Washington, D.C.: U.S. Government Printing Office.

We, the American elderly. (Number 10 in a series of reports from the 1970 Census). Washington, D.C.: U.S. Government Printing Office.

We, the first Americans. Washington, D.C.: U.S. Government Printing Office, 1973.

White House Conference on Aging. *Reports of the Special Concerns Sessions, 1971: The elderly Indian.* Washington, D.C.: U.S. Government Printing Office, 1972.

Youmans, E. G. Aging patterns in a rural and an urban area of Kentucky. *University of Kentucky Agricultural Experimental Station Bulletin,* 1963, No. 681.

UNPUBLISHED MATERIAL

Aberbach, J. D. *Alienation and race.* Unpublished doctoral dissertation, Yale University, 1968.

Acquino, V. R. *The Filipino Community in Los Angeles.* Unpublished master's thesis, University of Southern California, Los Angeles, 1952.

Agogino, George. *A study of the stereotype of the American Indian.* Unpublished master's thesis, University of New Mexico, 1950.

Antenor, J. A. *An exploratory study of the relation of the adjustment of 100 aged Negro men in Durham, North Carolina with their education, health and work status.* Unpublished master's thesis, North Carolina, 1961.

Ball, M. E. *Comparison of characteristics of aged Negroes in two counties.* Unpublished master's thesis, Howard University, Washington, D.C., 1966.

Barg, S. K., Kent, S. P., Hirsch, C., & Silverman, S. L. *From "N" to ego: Some program aspects in applied research.* Paper presented at the Annual Meeting of Gerontological Society, Denver, 1968.

Boggs, S. *The people of St. Louis, 1957.* St. Louis: Washington University, 1958.

Bohanon, T. *Some considerations of St. Louis' Negro aged.* Unpublished master's thesis, circa 1958.

Cameron, P. *Racial differences in contents of conscious.* In preparation, *1973.*

Carp, Francis. Factors in utilization of services by the Mexican-American elderly. Palo Alto, Calif.: American Institute for Research, 1968.

Chen, W. C. *Changing socio-cultural patterns of the Chinese community in Los Angeles.* Unpublished doctoral dissertation, University of Southern California, Los Angeles, 1952.

The Chicano elderly: The silent majority. Newsletter of the La Raza Information Center, January 1973.

Cho, C. S. *Correlation of cultural assimilation of two groups of Issei women.* Unpublished master's thesis, University of Washington, Seattle, 1953.

Collins, Bill, & Yee, Donna. *Social forces within the Seattle Filipino American community today: 1972.* Demonstration Project for Asian-Americans, Seattle, Washington, February 1972.

Conferences on improving services to aging Mexican Americans. Western Center Consultants, East Los Angeles, California, April 1969.

Crocker, M. W. *An analysis of the living arrangements and housing conditions of old age assistance recipients in Mississippi.* Unpublished doctoral dissertation, Florida State University, Tallahassee, 1968.

Cyrus-Lutz, Catherine, & Gaitz, Charles. *Lifetime Goals: Age and ethnic considerations.* Houston: Texas Research Institute of Mental Sciences, 1970.

Dare, R. K. *The economic and social adjustment of San Francisco Chinese for the past 50 years.* Unpublished master's thesis, University of California, Berkeley, 1959.

Davis, A., Jr. *Selected characteristic patterns of a southern aged rural Negro population.* Unpublished master's thesis, Washington, D.C., Howard University, 1966.

86   Davis, G. *The effects of the Social Security Act on the status Negro.* Unpublished doctoral dissertation, University of Iowa, Ames, 1939.

Deals, R. *Culture patterns of Mexican-American life.* Proceedings of the Fifth Annual Conference, Southwestern Conference on the Education of Spanish-speaking people, Los Angeles, January 1951.

Dhaliwal, D. D. *A sociological description and analysis of a non-random sample of low-income Washington, D.C. aged Negroes.* Unpublished master's thesis, Howard University, Washington, D.C., 1966.

Dieppa, Ismael. *Reaching the elderly poor through Project FIND: Implications for practice in voluntary and public agencies.* Paper presented at 95th Annual Forum, National Conference on Social Welfare, San Francisco, May 1968.

Final report of delivery services to the Tampa model citites aged: A demonstration project. University of Florida Aging Studies Program, Tampa, 1969-1972.

Gallegos, Eleuterio. *A community centered project for the Chicano aged.* Interstate Research Associates, Denver, Colorado, 1973.

Geagin, J. R. *The social ties of Negroes in an urban environment.* Unpublished doctoral dissertation, Cambridge, Massachusetts, Harvard University, 1966.

Gibson, Guadalupe, & Gomez, Ernesto. *El Centro del Barrio, Progress Report.* Worden School of Social Service, Our Lady of the Lake College, San Antonio, Texas, February 1973.

Gillespie, Michael. *The effect of residential segregation on the social integration of the aged.* Unpublished paper, University of Missouri, August 3, 1967.

Hamlett, M. L. *An exploratory study of the socioeconomic and psychological problems of adjustment of 100 aged and retired Negro women in Durham, North Carolina during 1959.* Unpublished master's thesis, North Carolina College, 1959.

Harper, D. W., Jr. *Socialization for the aged status among the Negro, French, and non-French sub-cultures of Louisiana.* Louisiana State University, 1967.

Harper, D. W., Jr., & Garza, J. M. *Ethnicity, family generational structure, and intergenerational solidarity.* Paper presented at the Annual Meeting of Gerontologial Society, Denver, 1968.

Henderson, G. *A study of aged Negroes receiving old age assistance.* Detroit: Detroit Urban League Community Service Department, December 1961.

Hill, Adenine. *A study of Michigan's Chicano population: Selected excerpts.* Unpublished.

Hirsch, G., Kent, D. P., & Silverman, S. L. *Homogeneity and heterogeneity among low-income Negro and white aged.* Paper presented at the 21st Annual Meeting of Gerontological Society, Denver, Colorado, November 1, 1968.

Jackson, Jacqueline J. *Changing kinship roles and patterns among older persons in a Black community.* Paper presented at the American Psychological Association, Washington, D.C., September 1, 1969.

Jackson, Jacqueline J. *Leisure-time activities of Negro men, aged forty-five through fifty-four.* Unpublished doctoral dissertation, Pennsylvania State University, 1955.

Jackson, Jacqueline J. *Leisure-time and mental outlook: A comparison of southern rural aged samples.* Unpublished master's thesis, 1967.

Jackson, Jacqueline J. *Retired Negroes: Some empirical findings and impressionistic judgments.* Paper presented at the Conference on Ethnic Differences in Patterns of Retirement. Tucson: The Adult Development and Aging Branch NICHD, 1969.

Kalish, Richard, & Reynolds, David. *The meaning of death and dying in the Los Angeles Mexican-American community.* Unpublished paper, December 1971.

Kanagawa, W. Y. *A study of old age assistance recipients of Japanese ancestry under Honolulu County Department of Welfare.* Unpublished master's thesis, University of Hawaii, 1955.

Kent, Donald P., & Hirsch, Carol. *Differentials in need and problem solving techniques among low-income Negro and white elderly.* Paper presented at the 8th International Congress of Gerontology, Washington, D.C., August 25, 1969.

Kimura, Y. *A comparative study of the collective adjustment of the Issei, the First generation Japanese in Hawaii and in Mainland United States since Pearl Harbor.* Unpublished doctoral dissertation, University of Chicago, 1952.

Kripalani, G. K. *Net migration response differentials by age, sex and color for the U.S.* Unpublished doctoral dissertation, University of Florida, 1967.

Lambing, M. A. *Study of retired older Negroes in an urban setting.* Unpublished doctoral dissertation, University of Florida, 1969.

Lee, David Y. *Report on Korean-American community in Los Angeles.* Demonstration Project for Asian American, Los Angeles, California, January 1972.

Lopata, H. *Social isolation of the lower-class blue collar woman.* Paper read at the Ohio Valley Sociological Society Meetings, Akron, Ohio, May 1970.

Lopez, Loretta. *Extended family patterns of Mexican-Americans.* A report on Chicano curriculum development. University of Denver Graduate School of Social Work, 1971-72.

Marian, H. *The Filipino immigrant in the U.S.* Unpublished master's thesis, University of Chicago, 1934.

Martinez, Homer. *The Mexican-American elderly.* National Council on Aging, 1971.

Mexican American Population in California. A report of the Mexican-American Population Commission of California, San Francisco, California, June 1973.

Minority Aged in America. (Papers from a Symposium Triple Jeopardy: The Plight of Aged Minorities. April 17, 1971), Detroit, Michigan: Institute of Gerontology, The University of Michigan-Wayne State University.

88   Moore, Joan. *The death culture of Mexico and Mexican-Americans.* Unpublished, 1970.

Nakagaki, M. *A study of marriage and family relationships among three generations of Japanese-American family groups.* Unpublished master's thesis, University of Southern California, 1964.

Nash, G., Lawton, M. P., & Simon, B. *Blacks and whites in public housing for the elderly.* Paper presented at the Annual Meeting of Gerontological Society, Denver, Colorado, 1968.

On the feasibility of training Asians to work with Asian elderly: A preliminary assessment of needs and resources available to Asian elderly in Seattle, Washington. Prepared by Training Project for the Asian Elderly—Glenn Chinn, Principal Investigator, March 1973.

Palmore, E. *The aged poor: Finds of Project FIND.* A report prepared for the National Council on Aging, New York, 1969.

Pettigrew, Thomas F. *The Negro aged: A minority within a minority.* Unpublished paper, Institute for State Executives in Aging, Brandeis University, 1967.

Preliminary statement of needs and design of a prototype center for services to the Puerto Rican aged in New York City. DMM Associates, 1973.

Ragan, Pauline. *Aging among Blacks, Mexican-Americans and Anglos—Problems and possibilities of research as reflected in the literature.* Los Angeles: Andrus Gerontology Center, USC, March 1973.

Raya, Arturo. *Social policy and the minority aging.* Institute on Minority Aging, School of Social Work, San Diego State University, June 1973.

Reich, J. M., Stegman, M. A., & Stegman, N. W. Relocating *the disposed elderly: A study of Mexican-Americans.* Institute for Environmental Studies, University of Pennsylvania, Philadelphia, 1966.

Reynolds, David K. *Attitudes and consequences of death-related behaviors in the Japanese-American community.* Unpublished paper, June 1970.

Reynolds, David K. *Japanese-American aging: A game perspective.* Paper presented at the Society for Applied Anthropology Meeting, Miami, Florida, April 16, 1971.

Roberts, R. E. *Ethnic and racial differences in the characteristics and attitudes of the aged in selected areas of rural Louisiana.* Unpublished master's thesis, Louisiana State University, 1964.

Ross, R. *Social distance between first and second generation Japanese in Los Angeles.* Unpublished master's thesis, University of Southen California, Los Angeles, 1939.

Rothman, Sandra M. *Legal services and the elderly Cuban.* Miami, Florida: Legal Services of Greater Miami, Inc.

Rubenstein, Daniel. *Social gerontology and Black people.* Unpublished paper.

Sánchez, Pablo. *The Spanish heritage elderly.* Paper presented at the Institute on Minority Aging, School of Social Work, San Diego State University, San Diego, June 1973.

Santiestivan, Henry. *Statement.* Text of remarks made before the Special Committee on Aging, U.S. Senate, November 21, 1969.

Schonfield, D., & Trimble, J. *Advantages of aging.* Paper presented at the 20th Annual Meeting of the Gerontological Society, St. Petersburg, Florida, 1967.

Sherman, E. G., Jr. *Social adjustment of aged Negroes of Carbondale, Illinois.* Unpublished master's thesis, Southern Illinois University, 1955.

Smith, S. H. *The Negro family.* Lecture, Duke University, 1967.

Smith, S. H. *The older Negro American.* Unpublished master's thesis, 1966.

Solomon, B. J. *Social functioning of economically dependent aged.* Unpublished DSW dissertation, School of Social Work, University of Southern California, August 1966.

The Spanish-speaking elderly poor. A report to the Office of Economic Opportunity Part I, April 1973. The Federation of Experienced Americans and the U.S. Human Resources Corporation.

Stanford, P. S. *Values of some Issei Japanese of Hanapepe Valley, Kauai.* Unpublished master's thesis, University of Hawaii, 1961.

Steglich, W. G. Cartwright, W. J., & Crouch, B. *Survey of needs and resources among aged Mexican-Americans.* Lubbock, Texas: Texas Technological College, 1968.

Stojanovic, E. J. *Moral and Its correlates among aged Black and white rural women in Mississippi.* Unpublished doctoral disserattion, State College, Mississippi State University, 1970.

Stone, V. *Personal adjustment in aging in relation to community environment, a study of persons sixty years and over in Carrbora and Chapel Hill, North Carolina.* Unpublished doctoral dissertation, University of North Carolina, 1959.

Stretch, J. J. *The development and testing of a theoretical formulation that aged Negroes with differences in community security are different in coping reactions.* New Orleans, La.: Tulane University, 1967.

Tamura, Fumi Yoshida. *A Cross-generational study of the attitudes toward the aging person and aging process and the acceptance of a home for the aged in the Japanese-American family.* Unpublished master's thesis, University of California, Los Angeles, 1969.

Tibbitts, C. *Middle-aged and older people in American society.* Paper reproduced by the Gerontological Society, Projects Division, with permission, from a paper prepared for the Training Institute for Public Welfare Specialist in Aging, Cleveland, Ohio, June 1965.

Thune, Jeanne M. *Group portrait in Black and white.* Nashville, Tenn.: Senior Citizens, Inc., 1969.

90   Torres-Gil, Fernando. *Los Ancianos de La Raza, a beginning framework for research, analysis, and policy.* Waltham, Mass.: Brandeis, University, May 1972.

Utile. A newsletter published by La Asociación, *Los Viejos Utiles,* Año I, Numeros 4, 5, 8, and Año II, Numeros 10, 11, 13, and 15.

Yanagita, Yuki. *Familial, occupational, and social characteristics of three generations of Japanese-Americans.* Unpublished master's thesis, University of Southern California, Los Angeles, 1968.

Yuen, S. *Aging and mental health in San Francisco's Chinatown. Ethnicity, Mental Health and Aging: Summary of Proceedings of a Two-Day Workshop.* Los Angeles: Ethel Percy Andrus Gerontological Center, University of Southern California, April 13-14, 1970.

APPENDICES

INPUT ON LEGISLATION

Sherron Heimstra, Chairperson

I.   The following is a list of valuable contacts at the federal level.

   A.   Senate Special Committee on Aging
      U.S. Senate, Room G-233
      Washington, D.C. 20201

      1.   Role:
   a   a.   Investigates and recommends, however has no legislative power
          b.   Publishes newsletter on current issues
             e.g.,   Multiple Hazards of Race and Age

      2.   Contacts:
          a.   Senator Frank Church, Chairperson
          b.   Val Halamandaris, Extended Care Facilities
          c.   George Cronin, Transportation and Housing
          d.   Debbie Kilmer, Supplemental Security Income

   B.   House Committee on Aging
      U.S. House of Representatives 20510

      1.   Role:
          a.   Investigates and recommends, however has no legislative power
          b.   Publishes newsletter on current issues
             e.g.,   Multiple Hazards of Race and Age

      2.   Contacts:
          a.   William Randel
          b.   Bob Wilson

   C.   Administration on Aging
      400 6th Street, Southwest
      Washington, D.C. 20201

      1.   Role:
          a.   Publishes current data pertaining to elderly
          b.   Publishes legislative updates

      2.   Contacts:
          a.   Dolores Cutler, Legislation
          b.   Clark Tibbitts, Public Information

   D.   Federal Council on Aging
      Room 4026
      400 6th Street, Southwest
      Washington, D.C. 20201

1. Role:
   a. Advocacy
   b. Conducts panel on current issues on aging with open hearings
   c. An independent council

2. Contacts:
   a. Cleo Tavini, Staff Director
   b. Bertha Adkins, Chairperson

E. Office of Special Concerns
   Department of Health, Education and Welfare
   330 Independence Avenue
   Washington, D.C. 20201

   1. Role:
      a. Looks at the programs of HEW across the board and analyzes its impact on the minority older persons

   2. Contacts:
      Write general office

F. Health Insurance Benefits Advisory Council
   Write to: Social Security Administration
             Department of Health, Education, and Welfare
             330 Independence Avenue
             Washington, D.C. 20201

   1. Role:
      a. Deals with health issues

   2. Contacts:
      a. Write general office

II. Publications coming out of some of the above committees are:

A. Index on Legislation
   Administration on Aging
   400 6th Street, Southwest
   Washington, D.C. 20201

   1. Contains:
      a. Basic summary on current legislation (by bill number and page)
      b. Information on the legislation and who introduced it
      c. List major changes in legislation (short paragraph form)

B. American Public Welfare Association

   1. Contains:
      a. Indices on the impact of upcoming budgets and their effect on welfare workers. This publication does not pertain directly to the elderly, however, it does give some indirect information on benefits to the elderly

(Publication can be obtained *free* from your Congressmen or Committee publishing them.)

III. Notes to Remember

A. Go directly to source with your concerns by first finding out who handles this area. (TIME is the important element here.)

B. You have more *impact* when representing an outside agency

C. Go to open hearings knowledgeable about your area of concern (facts and figures)

D. Use a state and federal *lobby* when possible

E. Invite a staff member from one of these committees to your community when they're considering an issue that will affect your *constituency*

F. Write letters, one page in length, containing *facts* and *force*

G. You can request hearings when none have been provided

H. Don't hesitate to raise issues

I. Use your contacts at the state and federal levels

IV. Current Research

A. TOPIC—*Specific Ethnic Groups by Age and Income*

B. Federal Contact:

Don Fowles
Office of Administration on Aging

C. Local Contact—by county

Phil Ragle, San Diego

THE LEGISLATIVE-POLICYMAKING PROCESS

WEDNESDAY, May 28, 1975

8:00 a.m.   Registration

9:00 a.m.   Opening Session

10:00 a.m.   Keynote Presentation: "Legislative Process and the Minority Elderly"

10:45 a.m.   Break

11:00 a.m.   Panel: "Sources of Significant Input for Legislation"
Governmental speakers from the national, state, and local level, as well as
the private sector, will discuss policy formulation and possible means for
the elderly input into the process of policy development.

12:30 p.m.   Luncheon Presentation: "Justice and the Ethnic Minority Elderly"

2:15 p.m.   Training Seminars
Led by the morning panelists
"How the Aged can Develop Strategies for Effective Policy Input at the
Different Levels of the Public and Private Sector"

3:45 p.m.   Break

4:00 p.m.   Summary Observations from Training Seminars

5:00 p.m.   Announcements and Adjournment

5:15 p.m.   Social Hour

THURSDAY, May 29, 1975

8:00 a.m.   Registration

9:00 a.m.   Announcements and Introductions

9:15 a.m.   Panel: "Overview of Current Policy Issues and the Effect on the
Minority Aged"
    Policy and the Minority Aged at the State Level"
    Model for Action in Health: Policy, Planning, and the Minority"Aged"
    Social Security and Supplemental Security Income"
    Research as it Relates to Policy Formation"

12:30 p.m.   Luncheon Presentation: To Be Announced

2:15 p.m.   Training Seminars
Directed by morning panelist

3:45 p.m.   Break

4:00 p.m.   Summary Observations from Training Seminars

5:00 p.m.   Announcements and adjournment

7:30 p.m.   Films and Discussion

FRIDAY, May 30, 1975

8:00 a.m.   Registration

9:00 a.m.   Announcements and Introductions

9:15 a.m.   To Be Announced

10:00 a.m.   "Implications of Current and Pending Health Legislation on the Minority Older Person"

10:45 a.m.   Break

11:00 a.m.   "Labor Relations and the Minority Elderly"

11:45 a.m.   "Public and Private Pension and Retirement Policies Effect on the Minority Aged"

12:30 p.m.   Luncheon Presentation: "Strategies for Affecting Legislative Priorities"

2:15 p.m.   Summary and Wrap-Up of Institute